The Accidental

The Accidental Pornographer

A story about having a go and succeeding ... in failing

GAVIN GRIFFITHS

CAPSTONE

John Wiley & Sons, Ltd

First published in 2008 by
Capstone Publishing Ltd. (a Wiley Company)
The Atrium, Southern Gate, Chichester, PO19 8SQ, UK.
www.wileyeurope.com
Email (for orders and customer service enquires): cs-books@wiley.co.uk

Other Wiley Editorial Offices
John Wiley & Sons Inc., 111 River Street, Hoboken, NJ 07030, USA
Jossey-Bass, 989 Market Street, San Francisco, CA 94103–1741, USA
Wiley-VCH Verlag GmbH, Boschstr. 12, D-69469 Weinheim, Germany
John Wiley & Sons Australia Ltd, 42 McDougall Street, Milton, Queensland 4064, Australia
John Wiley & Sons (Asia) Pte Ltd, 2 Clementi Loop #02–01, Jin Xing Distripark, Singapore 129809
John Wiley & Sons Canada Ltd, 22 Worcester Road, Etobicoke, Ontario, Canada M9W 1L1

A catalogue record for this book is available from the British Library

Library of Congress Cataloging-in-Publication Data
Griffiths, Gavin.
  The accidental pornographer / by Gavin Griffiths.
    p. cm.
  Includes index.
  ISBN 978-1-906465-25-4 (pbk. : alk. paper) 1. Griffiths, Gavin. 2. Publishers and publishing--Great Britain--Biography. 3. Erotic review. 4. Sex-oriented periodicals--Publishing--Great Britain--History--21st century. I. Title.
  Z325.G86G75 2008
  070.5092--dc22
  [B]

2008019032

ISBN: 978-1-90646-525-4

Typeset in Baskerville by Sparks, Oxford – www.sparkspublishing.com
Printed and bound in Great Britain by TJ International Ltd, Padstow, Cornwall

Substantial discounts on bulk quantities of Capstone Books are available to corporations, professional associations and other organizations. For details telephone John Wiley & Sons on (+44) 1243 770441, fax (+44) 1243 770571 or email corporatedevelopment@wiley.co.uk

For Mrs G

Contents

Foreword
by Rachel Elnaugh

Entrepreneur, original star of BBC TV's *Dragons' Den*
and author of *Business Nightmares*

We're all used to reading the carefully glossed up rags-to-riches stories of modern-day entrepreneurs which, although intended to be inspirational, usually leave the reader a little green with envy and generally rather sick about their own lot in life. So it's wonderfully refreshing to hear the honest story of someone who took the plunge, left their salaried job to go into business and then supremely fucked up.

Gavin Griffiths' tale of how he came to acquire an ailing business for £1 almost by accident, then experienced trial after tribulation, and finally be forced to sell it for not a huge amount more to one of the country's richest and most successful publishers 18 months later, is both endearing and at times hilarious.

Gavin's story illustrates the sad reality of enterprise in the UK today; the fact that, while the fortunate few will see their entrepreneurial dreams come true, the vast majority who launch into business will either fail or barely scratch a living. In this respect, going into business and expecting to become a Rich List multi-millionaire is for most as unrealistic as getting on a rollercoaster and expecting to get off some place different to where you started.

However, Gavin's story does illustrate that the fun of the entrepreneurial rollercoaster ride is often a far greater compensation. And that alone has to be a justification for at least giving it a shot. Then, if by some fluke you ALSO manage to get yourself rich along the way, you can view it as a huge life bonus!

Rachel Elnaugh
July 2008

Acknowledgements

There are many people I need to thank for being part of this story and in many cases being as instrumental in proceedings as I was. So here they are in order of appearance: My father, for encouraging me to have a crack and for the snippets of sound advice he drops without always knowing it; Don Smith, the CEO of eyestorm. com, for being a visionary, for proving how personal energy can move people and for giving me a break when I really needed it; Rowan, my partner, for choosing me, trusting me and sticking with me; Sally, for being a voice of reason and a source of great support in the difficult times; Annie, for making me laugh almost continuously and for being my first ever real employee; Pauline, for being an angel; Jamie Maclean, for selling me the magazine and making the very early days much easier than they should have been. Michael Carter, for so freely imparting advice and wisdom without ever really getting anything in return (twice). The Boys, for their investment and belief in our venture; Ian Leggett for the sheer sport and the amount of times he made me walk up and down Cleveland Street; Gordon Wise, my agent, for not giving up on this project when every one said, 'er, not really'. Behind this story is a wider cast of people who chipped in working for free or lunch or mates' rates and helped make all this possible; and, of course, let us not forget the *Erotic Review* readers who were there long before I was involved and remained there long after I left.

Introduction

Confession time: my name is Gavin Griffiths, and for over a year I was a pornographer. It's a simple story of boy meets girl, girl edits erotic magazine, boy quits job to join girl, girl and boy buy erotic magazine for a pound. But this is not a success story. At least not success in the way that most people define it. Business success is usually characterized in terms of starting with nothing – preferably with a wretched backdrop of grinding poverty where your family of 12 share a room in a tumbledown tenement – and through guile, ruthlessness and unlimited hard work you reach a point where you suddenly find yourself swimming in cash. The result of all this wealth is that everyone pats you on the back, your friends get jealous, you buy a country estate and for the rest of your life everyone agrees with what you say. Even when you are wrong.

We're used to worshipping national entrepreneurial heroes such as Richard Branson or the late Anita Roddick because they fought the odds that were stacked against them, broke through the barriers and turned themselves and their businesses into household names whilst, of course, making a significant fortune along the way. Well this isn't one of those success stories – we didn't make it work, I'm not a household name and I certainly didn't make my fortune.

But we did leave the pavilion and we took up position to bat and we had a go. During this time I saw my first child come kicking and screaming into the world and my beloved grandmother slowly lose her grip and then depart from this mortal coil. Both of these events took place in similar hospital rooms, with family close at hand, concerning people separated by almost 80 years. And this is what this book is all about. It's about having a go. It's about what I did with one of those allotted 80 years, a year that I will always remember. It's a year that money could not have bought, a year where I learnt more about business and people and myself than I did in all those years preceding it. It's a year where I failed but somehow managed to get a result of sorts. So if you don't mind stepping up to the crease with me, and being bowled out in the first over, then read on. If failure's not your cup of tea then may I suggest you swap this for *Losing My Virginity* by Richard Branson. Contrary to what you may have read in other books, not everyone can do it!

CHAPTER ONE

How to buy an erotic magazine for a pound

T riggers O'Grady was a novice pornographer and he was looking increasingly more uncomfortable as the photo shoot progressed. Thankfully, his lovely fiancée was downstairs styling the models otherwise he would never have been able to explain to her why he was spending the morning with a very tall semi-naked African glamour model. He had been a photographer since leaving college and found he was rather good at doing dogs. He dipped into fashion occasionally but it didn't pay too well as there were too many other people doing it for nothing just to get their big break. Most people think fashion photographers are terrifically well paid and glamorous, but the reality is that most of them earn less than a checkout girl. Although it has to be said that they probably have more fun and they don't have to face the daily risk of 'checkout back' or repetitive strain injury. The dog market was, in contrast, underserviced and he was making a tidy, albeit niche, living by indulging wealthy pooch lovers. He once did a shot of a very sexy black Labrador wearing a solitary black stiletto and this is where I had come across him. On asking if he fancied participating in a new, adult business venture he jumped at the chance. He was eager to share in the vast wealth that pornography purports to generate but was reluctant to destroy the clean-cut image that he'd worked so hard to create amongst the Crufts set. So he agreed to help me, but only if he could work under a pseudonym; and thus, Triggers was born.

I didn't know too much about the sex industry either, and Triggers and I threw nervous looks at each other across the room as the models I had hired started to strip off and change into their stockings and basques in front of us. I had once seen a TV documentary where the film crew recorded scenes backstage at a London top-end fashion show and all the models walked around half-naked wearing only their miniscule underwear and shreds of costume. This shoot was nothing like that. There was a considerable absence of supermodels, wealth or glamour. They were an odd mix. One was seventy years old and lived on Sloane Square. Another was Australian, quite pretty and informed us she had a rash. One girl called Blade, from Tottenham, told us she was an African princess. Which she wasn't.

Nicole from France was up first. We had hired a grand house in the not so grand Mile End district of East London and it was costing me £100 per hour so we needed to get a shift on. We were using various rooms in the house to do the shoot and the girls were supposed to strip for Triggers and he would photograph them. We would be using the photos for a website I was planning to launch later that week. Triggers led Nicole up to the first floor and into the white room. I waited at the bottom of the stairs not quite knowing what to do. Having never directed a nude erotic photo shoot before I wasn't sure if I was supposed to be in the room while Nicole stripped and nobody was giving me any hints on the correct porn-shoot etiquette. I had briefed Triggers fully, so opted for the gentlemanly approach, stayed out of the room and waited for the shoot to finish.

I sat on the bottom step, lit up a fag I'd bummed from Blade, coughed, put it out because I don't smoke and in a quiet moment of reflection wondered how I had got into all this. How had I ended up surrounded by semi-naked glamour models running a porn shoot in Mile End? How had a respectable, strait-laced shipping executive managed to stray so far from everything he knew? I had no real intention or ambition to get into the 'adult' business and if anything I consider myself to be a bit of a prude. Before I continue with my sleazy story now might be an opportune time to fill in a few blanks and set the scene as to how all this came about.

In my twenties I did a very sensible job in the shipping industry. Not exactly a high flyer but I had big plans. I worked with a great team of people and had travelled to far-off places and suppose I really could have done a lot worse. Then, for no apparent reason, shortly after my thirtieth birthday I decided my life had to take a different course. I felt a desperate, powerful yearning to do something different, something off the wall, something crazy, something risky. I wanted to make a difference to the world, make my mark, create something on my own. It was as if a switch had been flicked and I knew that at least I had to have a go at finding that 'thing' before I was trapped by kids' school fees and life insurance. So I left the colleagues who were like family, and the comfort and security of job I had done for most of my adult life, and I stepped hesitantly out into the abyss.

So it was that on 1 August 2000 I awoke to find myself without any important stuff to do. Number one priority was to find this fabled dream job promptly as I had just enough money in the bank to cover the mortgage at the end of the month and didn't relish the prospect of living off my wife, Katharine, who I had married only a month before. I'm sure when she had signed up to the 'for richer or poorer' bit she had not expected to be putting that particular vow into practice only a few short weeks after returning from our honeymoon. We had recently purchased a run-down house in Bethnal Green, in London's rough East End, with a view to ripping it all out and doing it up, which was all the rage at the time amongst middle class south-west Londoners. We had thrown ourselves into the ripping out bit with gusto and then the project had sort of lost momentum somewhat as jobs and weekend hangovers took over, along with the realization that plastering is actually impossible and that re-wiring electrics is best left to experts because electric shocks really hurt. With my new unemployed status the renovations had come to a complete standstill until the income tap was switched back on again. So I sat at the kitchen table, surrounded by half-finished DIY projects, wires dangling from the ceiling, job section and pen in hand and started to hunt for jobs.

I began my journey in the Appointments section of the *Sunday Times*. I rather fancied new media. More than a rational desire to enter the internet world I think that the sector entitled 'new media' was about as far from shipping as I could possibly get. It was *'new'* (excellent), and in *'media'* (marvellous), so surely it must be a bottomless pit of fun. Also, in an embarrassing display of shallowness, I was imagining dinner party scenarios:

Other Guest: 'So what do you do, Gavin?'

Gavin: 'I [pause] am in new media.' [Raises right eyebrow]

Other Guest looks seriously impressed and quite possibly a bit jealous.

Gavin 1, Other Guest nil.

CVs were duly dispatched and promptly resulted in three job interviews.

The first company was not strictly new media but they had included this all important phrase in the job advert to make it sound a lot more interesting than it was. It seems they had pioneered a way of making cereal packet inserts more exciting so I suppose in one respect they were 'new'. And if you really look at it cereal packet advertising is sort of 'media', just not very exciting media. Desperate for work I showed a distinctly awe-inspiring degree of enthusiasm for their cereal packet decoder and was not surprised when I was invited back for a second interview. In round two I had to prove to the management of this company that I was up to the job and that I could sell a concept. So a week later I was to be found doing a presentation about myself to the whole company and expressing why I wanted to get into cereal packet marketing. I found out two days later that they wanted me for the job but I just couldn't bring myself to take it. It was impossible to get worked up about the venture and I needed something that would make me fizz with enthusiasm. Something that would change my life.

The second company was a genuine new media company who were trying to create internet hubs. To this day I don't really understand what an internet hub is or what exactly they were trying to do with them. In hindsight I'm not even sure they knew what they were trying to do. I was confused further when two days before my interview they asked me to prepare a presentation on the state of English cricket which I would have to deliver to the board of directors. Today I would never go through such a preposterous exercise but back then I would have learnt to juggle and done roly-polys for a company Audi, £30k a year and a job in new media.

Other Guest: 'So what car do you drive, Gavin?'

Gavin: 'Oh, it's an Audi A4. Metallic silver. Auto. Aircon. Passenger Airbag.'

Full time score: Gavin 2, Other Guest nil.

I stood laden with anxiety in front of a board of very self-important men who seemed to consist of two Irish builders, an ex-sales manager from a calculator company and an angry young man with spiky hair who looked all of fifteen. I told them all about my rather bleak outlook for the future of English cricket. It was only later that I learnt how the dot-com industry had thrown up so much investment money, and had grown so quickly, that totally unsuitable people found themselves in utterly unviable businesses doing jobs they knew nothing about. You could have thought up the most ludicrous business proposition, put '.com' after it, called up some investors and stood back and let greed take over …

Internet Entrepreneur: 'Yeah, right, OK right, yeah, I've got this brilliant idea, right, for an internet venture called plonkerwonker.com.'

Investor: 'What does it do?'

Internet Entrepreneur: 'We're not sure yet but it'll sell *stuff*. Probably clothes. Or building supplies.'

Investor: 'What's the burn rate?'

Internet Entrepreneur: 'About £2 mil per month, but we get it up and running quickly and go to IPO by June and everyone's quids in.'

Investor: 'Who do I make the cheque payable to?'

… and that's how it worked. Seasoned investors and gullible pensioners alike pumped their cash into businesses that went bust within months.

The spiky haired boy, who turned out to be the chairman, asked me what I could bring to the company and I told him that I could bring passion and commitment, yup, definitely passion and commitment. I didn't get the job and out of curiosity six months later looked up the site and it didn't seem to exist. Perhaps hubs didn't take off in the end.

The third and final job was for a company called eyestorm. com. I went along to meet the boss of this start-up company who were going to sell top class modern art online. I was almost orgasmic at the prospect of being in art *and* in new media. I was one of five people going for the job as a sales executive. The chief executive was a powerhouse, full of energy and informed me of this gap in the market into which he was going to smash his wedge and break it wide open. It was a very impressive introduction. In typical dotcom fashion the company had started in one office and as they secured more funding the business had grown until such time that they had three offices on separate floors of a converted piano factory in Kentish Town, North London. During the course of my interview we were moved three times as people had reserved various corners of the building for meetings. Meetings didn't happen around desks with chairs like in the shipping industry, everyone seemed to be having loud and chatty meetings perched on boxes, or steps or anywhere where you could lodge a buttock. There was a thrilling, vibrant buzz about the place. Pretty girls were talking to each other and programmers walked past in flips-flops and string vests.

They had persuaded investors to give them $20 million to start a company that was going to break down the barriers of the art world. The boss and his team of 50 people were going to bring art to the masses. They were going to make the internet do to art what the phonograph had done with music: take it out of stately homes and public venues and let everyone have it at home. They had some of the best artists in the world signed up to the concept and they were going to employ the best people to make it happen. The job I wanted was in a new department which was going to sell contemporary art into offices, spreading the word on another front – not only giving people art at home but bringing it to the workplace. I would have started there and then if the boss had asked me. It was the antithesis of the shipping business, it represented everything that my last job had not given me with the added bonus that I could wear a string vest to work.

My enthusiasm for the position must have clearly swung it as I got the job and started selling contemporary art on 1 September 2000.

Now I know you might think I'm dragging my heels a bit on this. I'm not getting onto the porn bit or the failure bit. Eyestorm.com deserves a book all on its own – and that's for someone else to write – but I have to tell you about it because it shaped the way I began to think and it was directly responsible for me accidentally becoming a pornographer. So bear with me.

That first morning I was given a brand new, state-of-the-art laptop, a mobile phone, a pack of business cards (where I learnt that I was to be an acquisitions consultant), an email address and an Allen key. We had taken over another office in the basement and I was shown to an empty space in the corner where a flat-packed desk was propped against the wall. My first job was to construct my desk and go and find a chair. At lunchtime I was rather perturbed to see three young girls leaving the office crying.

At the end of my first day the whole company was summoned to a meeting. Everyone squeezed into one room and rather predictably sat on the floor or anywhere but on a chair and the important decisions and new strategies were announced. There was cause for celebration this particular day as the management had secured another several million dollars of funding which meant that the company didn't have to go bust that weekend. Hooray. But there was going to be some cost-cutting and it was regrettable that three of the lowest paid secretarial staff had been sacked that morning. Boo. But to cheer everyone up there was going to be an all expenses big black tie party in a horror-themed restaurant the following Thursday. Hooray. Welcome to the first dotcom boom, where the pain of cost-cutting is made bearable by throwing a party, the cost of which probably exceeds the three lowly secretarial salaries you've just saved.

The company continued to spend vast sums of money. We did shows, competitions, and advertised everywhere we could. In six months we had three separate marketing directors come through the business. For one week we booked huge adverts from one end of the platform to the other on the northbound Victoria Line at Oxford Circus. We did promotions, partnership deals, sponsored talks and threw parties. We had to reach a critical mass of sales to try to obtain the next round of funding. My immediate boss hired a limousine and four look-a-like models at £1000 each per day to drive around London mainline railway stations dishing out catalogues. This exercise cost thousands of pounds and did not generate one single sale. But we didn't care, we were making it up as we went along because nobody had done this before. If you had an idea, you brought it to the table and if they liked it you 'owned it and ran with it'. If it flopped you would console yourself with the phrase 'yeah, but it's good brand building'. Money was flying out the door and the whole building vibrated with enthusiasm as we missed our sales targets week in week out. Profit was a word rarely mentioned, but the spectre of profit, or rather lack of it, could be seen on the faces of the finance team who were watching the cash melt rapidly away. The hottest topic around the water coolers was the speculation on when the next round of funding was due to come in.

The latest buzz words in the dotcom business were 'clicks and mortar'. This is the ironic trend for companies that had championed the benefits of the virtual marketplace over the traditional physical world developing physical embodiments for their businesses. Desperate to find ways of spending our seemingly limitless supply of investor funds we opened an art gallery in London's West End and had a huge party to celebrate. It was boom time. This was the most fantastic working time in my life and going to the office in the morning was a total thrill.

For the first time I felt as if I was in my right groove. I belonged here in this company and I was playing an important role. I had been noticed by the CEO and had been given a few promotions and after nine months I was running the customer services operation. But there was still a nagging feeling that something wasn't quite right. From my new position I could see that the company's income was minimal and totally disproportionate to the massive outgoings. Despite encouragement from the management it was hard to see how long this could go on for. More unsettling still was the little voice in the back of my head that told me I should be working for myself. It was like an irksome demon ever so quietly nagging me every day – and I knew that no matter how much I tried to ignore it, it would not go away. It wanted me to answer to no one. It wanted me to be someone.

By April I was utterly exhausted. I was working long hours and most weekends. An old family friend invited us to Antigua, where he lives, for a holiday. This would be a cheap break in one of the most beautiful settings in the world, and I jumped at the chance.

Antigua is a tax haven and many internet companies had set up their offshore banking facilities there. I happened to meet a few wheeler-dealers while I was in a beach bar and one of them had made a fortune out of gambling. He informed me that to make money out of the internet I needed to either get into porn or gambling. Remember this bit for later, it's important. Porn and Gambling. P&G.

The first seed was sown and I intended to go back to London and try to get the company to develop an erotic art section to capitalize on this lucrative porn-led sector of the market.

While I was away there had been a bloodbath in the office with sackings and large-scale reorganization. I was pleased to discover that I had been promoted again and found myself now employed as Head of Sales for Europe. Suddenly I had people working for me, lots of responsibility and the London gallery was now under my control. I took to spending Fridays working there as it was on Maddox Street in the middle of the West End, and it dovetailed nicely with my social life as I liked to go out with my chums in Soho after it closed. In the afternoon I would run a lunch club where we would buy in some posh nibbles and crack open a few bottles of wine for rich business people in the area and try to flog them some art. We always found that getting people a bit pissed helped their barriers drop and enabled them to engage with the images more. Plus it made flogging the stuff easier. My life had changed beyond recognition in a year and now Friday afternoons were spent in a drunken fog of cold chardonnay waffling on about contemporary British art. If ever you find yourself in an art gallery and are worried about what to say when presented with anything large and abstract I find the best course of action is as follows:

Pause.

Cup your chin in your thumb and forefinger.

Pause again, breathe slowly and say: 'Hmmm, the ultimate nihilistic statement', and then move on.

One day the legendary artist Damien Hirst made an impromptu visit to the gallery. He was one of the artists on our roster and we always welcomed their participation in promoting the business. Damien asked if he could do an installation piece for us in the front window and naturally we said yes. He screwed up bits of paper, left half a cup of coffee, a sandwich crust, a beer bottle, paint brushes and an easel displaying one of his famous dot paintings. The installation was supposed to be a mock up of his gallery and the art students in the company were wetting themselves. I thought it looked like a pile of junk in the corner of the room but my artistic opinion was rarely asked for. It was rumoured that uber-collector Charles Saatchi was going to buy it for £100,000 for his own gallery. Everyone was thrilled to bits. So you can imagine my alarm the next morning when one of the girls from the gallery called me with some bad news regarding the installation. It seems that Abraham the cleaner had mistakenly thought it was the result of one of our raucous parties and had taken it upon himself to clean up the whole front window and put it in black bin bags on the pavement ready for collection. I called up one of the founders of the business and told him the news. He in turn rang Damien to see what was the best course of action. Damien, who was distinctly rock 'n' roll at that stage in his career, was indisposed having supposedly had magic mushrooms for breakfast and therefore unavailable for comment, or at least comment that would provide some sort of meaningful solution to our predicament. I sent one of my most artistic customer service lads down to the gallery armed with photos of the installation that were taken the previous day. He carefully removed the contents from the bin bags and painstakingly reconstructed the whole front window and everyone breathed a sigh of relief. Then I had a call from the *Sun* who had picked up the story from the owner of Abraham's cleaning firm who had cheerfully phoned in the details. This amusing anecdote was an irresistible *Sun* story and 'Is modern art rubbish?' predictably appeared on page five the next day.

We managed to secure yet another round of funding and this time as a member of the management team I learnt that, had we not secured it, the payroll would not have gone through that month. The simple fact was that this company was spending a very large amount of money. In the internet world it's called 'high burn'. I've always thought this turn of phrase odd. Having run my own business I would never talk about money in such a crude way. Money is the blood of a business, why would you want to burn it? Dotcom logic dictates that you throw massive amounts of money around in order to grab market share, which in turn provides the company with a high valuation so that you can sell your shares and buy an island. Profit is something that can be sorted out later by the team of mugs who have purchased the company from you. Unfortunately, a high burn rate with a low level of sales income means you run out of money very quickly indeed. Our regular injections of cash from investors were not going to go on for ever and so we implemented a programme of cost-cutting measures. I had to choose two people to let go from my department, and one Monday morning a whole squadron of people were made redundant. In my heart I knew that I could be the next redundancy and that this fantastic voyage could come to an end for me at any time.

It was at this time that I really started to work on my erotic art theory and I was introduced to The Erotic Print Society – a company run by two ex-art dealers called Jamie Ma-cLean and Tim Hobart. Jamie was an instantly likeable man with a relaxed air and a self-deprecating sense of humour. Tim, whilst also very amiable, seemed slightly cross and a bit distracted. I had arranged to meet them to talk about developing some erotic photography and during lunch they mentioned that they owned a magazine called the *Erotic Review* which was for sale. It seemed they were going through some restructuring. Their investors wanted them to strip the company back to its core business of mail order and stop fooling around with this magazine, which seemed to do nothing other than suck up a lot of money. The publication was a literary erotic magazine which was read largely by educated male fifty-somethings. It contained few pictures – with an emphasis on the written word accompanied by highly explicit line drawings, sketches and artistic photography. I thought it was a brilliant and original idea. It was rude and sexy without being porn. It was intelligent and you could see that it made sex acceptable. They wanted £100,000 for the title, staff and intellectual property and I said I would see if I could get my company to buy it. Unsurprisingly, Eyestorm was not too keen on purchasing an ailing publishing venture whilst trying to get to grips with its own art venture.

That Thursday we threw a particularly drunken party to celebrate a new hang at the gallery and I invited The Erotic Print Society (EPS). We had converted the basement into an erotic space and curated a show using all the erotic art we had in the Eyestorm portfolio. Once again we got talking about the magazine. I was getting more and more excited about the *Erotic Review* and I starting to think seriously about how I could purchase the magazine myself. The first dotcom phenomenon had created a hotbed of entreprencurialism throughout the developed world. It's easy to look back and laugh at the excesses, of which there were many, but the energy that underpinned it was driven from my generation taking a step into the limelight and having a go. It did not matter where you came from; providing you had a good idea and passion, you could get rich. You could do anything you wanted and, like thousands of others at the time, I believed I could be a contender. If I could find the right idea.

That night I was also introduced to Rowan Pelling, the eccentric editor of the magazine. I was slightly taken back on meeting Rowan as I had assumed having a man's name she would be a man. Rowan breezed into the room in all her feminine glory and I instantly liked her. Later Rowan was to write about our meeting in her weekly column in the *Independent on Sunday* where she described our first encounter akin to love at first sight. There was certainly some kind of connection, a feeling of trust you rarely find occurring so instantaneously. She had an easy manner, an incredibly 'jolly hockey sticks' posh accent and an attitude that was positively brimming with contagious enthusiasm.

We agreed to meet at noon the following day in the gallery. She told me all about the history of the magazine, how she had taken the reins from the founder, Jamie MacLean, nurtured it for years and how the EPS boys were using the proceeds from the magazine to support their mail-order enterprise. The exact opposite to the EPS boys' opinions on the subject. She thought it desperately unfair that her magazine was going to be sold from under her and what she really needed was a business partner who she could team up with and buy the magazine herself. It really was a perfect match. A lunchtime bottle of Pinot Grigio was buzzing around my head and I must have made the right noises as it was almost implied that I would take on the role and Rowan started talking about what 'we' had to do to relaunch. It started to look like the idea for my big break might have found me.

By November things at Eyestorm were looking fairly bleak. Suppliers were being paid late and there was an air of desperation. I knew that the time was right to set up this new business and I had to find a way of making it happen. The EPS boys were pressing Rowan to come up with the money or they were going to sell the magazine to the highest bidder. By now it was September and I discovered that it had not been published since June and there was a very real risk if it was left much longer that there would not even be a magazine to buy. If you don't publish for a few months you may as well throw in the towel. As time ticked by the EPS boys got more and more anxious. However, I could see no way of them selling the publication without Rowan so they were almost obliged to do business with us if they wanted to offload the title. Repeated threats and deadlines were missed. Still they kept coming back to me and it became obvious that despite the threat of other bidders the reality of the situation was that we were the only donkey in the derby.

Rowan and I started talking about how we could save the publication on an almost daily basis. In truth I wasn't entirely sure how I was going to do this. I was only just making my way in the art world and I knew nothing about publishing at all. One rainy Tuesday night she asked if I wanted to come and meet the team in the Academy Club.

It did occur to me at this stage that I was getting in a little deeper than I had first anticipated. It's all well and good getting pissed in an art gallery and throwing around a few ideas to a damsel in distress but now I was meeting the team and it all started to feel a bit serious. Meeting the *ER* team was quite frightening – something akin to meeting your prospective mother-in-law for the first time – but to the power of ten.

It was pouring it down in Soho and it took me half an hour to find the club. Eventually, through the rain, I came to this little nondescript black door on Lexington Street in Soho. ACADEMY CLUB was written unobtrusively under the buzzer as if they really didn't want people to know about the place. The intercom crackled and I could hear what sounded like a loud party going on in the background. I spoke hesitantly and was invited to walk up a flight of wobbly stairs that looked as if they dated back 300 years. They did actually date back 300 years. On the first level was another black door through which I left the silence of the landing and entered a scruffy, noisy, dimly lit, smoky little room with a bar in one corner. Squeezed into this tiny space were dozens of totally pissed writers. Welcome to the Academy Club, the unofficial home of the *ER*.

Rowan was late and so were the rest of the team I was supposed to meet. Sat in the corner was a sinister-looking man in his early thirties with the most unbelievable handlebar moustache I have ever seen. He was dressed in a vintage three piece suit and when I walked in he stood to attention and introduced himself in an accent so upper class that it seemed as if he could hardly be bothered moving his lips. I had difficulty understanding what he was saying and tried to be polite. I was offered a glass of wine and he told me that he and Rowan had been trying to save the magazine for over a year and so he was glad I was getting involved. He was twirling his moustache and suggesting ways that 'we' could save the magazine. Alarm bells immediately started to ring. How many people were there exactly trying to rescue this magazine? Had Rowan been doing the damsel in distress act to every cat in town?

My unease was quickly forgotten when the *ER* team burst into the club. Rowan, breezing in as usual in a flurry of apologies for lateness, was followed by Annie Blinkhorn. Annie was the diminutive deputy editor and Rowan's right-hand girl. Annie was followed by Dea, the assistant editor who was Annie's right-hand girl. Will was responsible for designing the magazine. Finally there followed a man in his mid-50s called Chris Peachment who was known as 'the editor on the loose' (whatever that meant). He had a continual look of bemusement on his face and gave off the distinct impression that he would rather be at home with his pipe and slippers.

'So,' said Annie, 'are you going to save us?'

Everyone stopped talking and looked at me.

Suddenly this was no longer a game. I gulped and muttered that I would do my best and the conversation moved on to nipple clamps. Clearly the team thought that everything was going to work out all right now that I was on board so we drank several bottles of celebratory claret and I started to convince myself that Rowan and I could actually make this happen.

Then next day, groggy with hangover, I decided that I could not play around with this anymore. I had to either go for it or stop talking about it. 'Piss or get off the pot' as they say in tough-guy movies. I met Rowan that night after work and we started to formulate a plan and actually put some numbers down on a piece of paper for the first time. In my naivety I thought we would need at least £100,000 to relaunch the title and we had to find a wealthy investor to make this happen. The reality of it was that we needed five times this amount but I'll come onto that a little later. We also needed to take control of the title from the EPS so that they would not sell it behind our backs. I also aired my concerns about too many cooks trying to save this particular broth.

Rowan mentioned that her sister-in-law, Sally, knew some stuff about marketing and would be interested in participating. Our conversation went on late and eventually I got home at about 11 p.m. My wife Katharine was still awake and I burst into the lounge and told her that tomorrow I was going to quit Eyestorm and buy the *Erotic Review*.

She replied, 'That's great news, darling, I'm pregnant.'

This information did change things considerably and I suggested that perhaps with a baby on the way I should exercise caution and not throw away a well paid job to re-launch an erotic magazine with a woman I had only just met. Katharine suggested that perhaps now was the right time to embark on such a project as when she was older she would want her children to go to good schools, to live in a lovely house and take nice holidays but for the next couple of years we could get away with taking the risk and being a bit broke. I'll never forget going to bed that night and holding my pregnant wife. It was the very essence of what life is about and I knew that with Katharine behind me I could achieve anything I wanted.

I didn't sleep well that night. My brain was overloaded with thoughts and lists of things that needed to be done. It was quite a conundrum. Before we did anything we needed to take control of the magazine as without it there was no deal to be done. Then we needed to get the team in place to put together and promote the magazine. This needed to be quickly followed by cash to pay everyone, particularly the printer who was going to print the thing and make our dream a reality. But we had no money so putting everything together was practically impossible. It seemed like an endless chicken and egg scenario except we had neither chicken nor egg.

The next morning I sat in my office at Eyestorm, rang Rowan, and we drew up a plan of attack. My first call was to Tim and Jamie of the EPS to arrange a meeting to discuss how we were going to buy the magazine. This seemed like the key element and I needed to start somewhere. It was a Monday and our weekly management meeting had droned on late as usual. By the time I left the office I was running half an hour late and I arrived at the EPS offices hot and harassed. The lift was broken so I had to run up eight flights of stairs, which left me gulping for air, and I entered the EPS offices very much on the back foot. Jamie and Tim had invited their lawyer along to play bad cop. Jamie and Tim played nice cop and slightly cross cop respectively. Rowan and I sat at one end of the table and they sat at the other. The atmosphere was tense, exacerbated by my lateness and general heavy breathing, sweating and spluttering.

The lawyer had a very serious look on her face and handed out four sets of documents called heads of agreement. This sort of document determines the shape of the deal and lays out what each party wants. You can actually use the heads of agreement as a contract when all terms are agreed to proceed with the sale.

Most of the paperwork was fairly innocuous and we agreed many of the clauses immediately. The main sticking point was the price of the magazine which was rather ambitiously set at £100,000. We suggested we pay one pound which, given there were no other buyers, seemed a perfectly realistic price for a practically bankrupt magazine. They quickly but unconvincingly retorted with £10,000 and once again we parried with our generous offer of one pound. In all the negotiations took minutes and finally we all agreed on the magic one pound figure. We also agreed that we would take on liabilities to the tune of £30,000 which were debts owed to a myriad of suppliers and contributors. There was also a ludicrous clause which stated that if we ever made more than £100,000 then the EPS could claim a ten per cent share. I'm not sure who thought up this one but Rowan instantly rejected it with a dismissive laugh.

We plodded through the rest of the agreement, tweaking it as much as possible in our favour and by the end we had a document that required almost no upfront payment at all. We now had time to think about the next step which was to secure financial backing with which to run our newly acquired magazine business.

We shook on the deal and Tim insisted that we sign it there and then to prevent them from going to any last minute bidders. I was willing to bet that there was nobody else lined up and I was reluctant to sign up to this agreement personally without the protection of a limited company which I had remembered from my Commerce O level about 13 years before. We stood our ground and it was agreed that we would meet in a week to sign the contracts and hand over the one pound.

That night I got home weary and worried. I had verbally agreed to go into this deal and there was no backing out. What had started out as a bit of a drunken joke had actually turned into a serious venture. In the shipping industry there is an old phrase which has been used by generations of brokers since they used to meet the merchant ships out at sea in their long boats: 'My word is my bond'. I had shaken hands on this deal and there was no way I was going back on it now.

The next step was to form a limited company to provide ourselves with a financial safeguard. A limited company, unlike a sole trader or partnership, offers a degree of protection which means that if your company goes bust, your liability as a director and shareholder is limited to the amount you put into the company in the first place. In our case we started the business with £10 share capital using an online company which specializes in incorporating limited companies. By setting up this business Rowan and I could sign up to the agreement but if we failed to secure funding we could effectively walk away from the whole deal, and the £30k worth of liabilities, without losing more than a fiver each.

By the end of the week The Erotic Review Limited was created. I left work early that afternoon and met up with Rowan. I had also asked my dad to meet us and give us some advice on the contract that we were about to sign. Although I was confident that we had negotiated good terms I wanted a seasoned businessman to have one last look before we signed our lives away. This was also the first time that I met Sally Pelling, Rowan's sister-in-law, who was coming on board as our marketing director. It turned out that Sally did indeed know 'some stuff' about marketing and had been a senior marketing manager at Sky which was going to come in handy when it came to selling the magazine to punters once we got cracking. Sally was calm and collected and from the moment she started talking I instantly felt she was right for the team. There was a brilliant dynamic: Rowan, the charismatic creative force, Sally, the sensible one who knew how to market our product and then me, the guy who would hopefully bring everything together, look after the money and make it happen. It was all so simple; we were going to be millionaires by this time next year and I would be snapping at Richard Branson's tail as a famous business leader, feted throughout the land, burdened with requests to open municipal buildings and do talks at black tie dinners about how savvy I was.

We met in a room above the Academy Club, which by coincidence belonged to the EPS lawyer. Here we signed what seemed like thousands of pieces of paper. After signing we all shook hands and the lawyer asked for one pound. I thought this was some kind of joke and Rowan and I laughed at the thought of having to hand it over. The lawyer was not laughing. Rowan only had £20 notes so I handed over the coin and the deal was done. We all trooped downstairs to the club to celebrate and to this day Rowan still owes me that 50p.

It turned into quite a drinking session. I remember hazily talking to some writer about my passion for Genghis Khan and behind me could hear Annie asking my dad if he ever wore a cock ring. My brother turned up with one of his work buddies who seemed bemused by the fact that his colleague's brother had accidentally purchased an erotic magazine for a pound.

My dad and brother and I decided to leave the club and go and have some dinner. It was a surreal night. I now owned an erotic magazine. I'll never forget those fatherly words of wisdom that night when he said that once you make that big step and work for yourself things will never be the same. I had thrown off the shackles of employment and in no time at all would be attending charity luncheons with Rupert Murdoch.

Except I hadn't got round to technically removing those shackles because I was still employed. All this was happening right under the nose of my existing employer and I was starting to worry that someone was going to find out that I was moonlighting. I still had a brilliant relationship with the management and a key role in the business only now I was the legal owner of an erotic magazine which I was running on the side. I didn't want to get found out and sour my relationship with people I respected and I knew that the only real way my new venture was going to work was to resign and go and work on it full time. If I stayed at Eyestorm the magazine was going to be a plaything.

So in early November I asked my managing director if I could have a quiet word with her and we arranged to meet near the skip outside the office. It was obvious what was coming and she hugged me and said she didn't know what she was going to do without her number two. It was a very sad moment.

Later that week we had one of our monthly meetings where the chief executive gave a pep talk and announced what was happening in the business. Second on the agenda was the news that I was leaving the business. The die was now cast and there was no turning back. We agreed that I would formally leave at the end of December but that I would work for a further two months on two days a week as a consultant until the end of February. Much to my surprise eyestorm.com never did fold and managed to keep afloat until new management took over in 2006. I am pleased to see the company appears to be going from strength to strength and last time I visited the Tate Modern I was delighted to see they had opened a branch right outside the Turbine Hall.

For my part, all I had to do now was find some money to relaunch the magazine.

CHAPTER TWO

Erotic Towers

By now it was early December and there was going to be a lot of work required to turn around the fortunes of this ailing little magazine. I decided that we needed a team meeting and assembled the gang in the EPS offices where the magazine and staff were squatting until we found a new home. The offices of the *ER*, or Erotic Towers as they were known, were like nothing I had ever seen. The building housing the office was on the third floor of a grand Edwardian block which looked straight out onto Regent Street. From the exterior it looked like the sort of place you might find a rather strait-laced Mayfair merchant bank full of duffers wearing braces and talking about murdering wildlife at weekends. Inside it looked like it had been ransacked by a gang of German perverts. Nobody ever seemed to throw anything away and it resembled the contents of a deviant's squat rather than an office where people actually worked. It was awash with books, filthy magazines, sex toys, lingerie, fruit, erotic artwork and photography and, peculiarly, several loose toilet rolls. There were clothes hung from every available nook and cranny. One small section of the room seemed to be kept in rigid order and this was the spot occupied by Chris Peachment, who I had discovered was an ex-RAF test pilot and perpetually looked halfway between rather cross and ever so slightly confused.

Chris was the only person in our fledgling organization that had ever worked for a magazine for any amount of time. He hadn't been paid since the summer but kept coming into the office out of habit. Chris is a class act, a journalist of the old school and if you brush away the gruff exterior underneath is a very funny man. He believes in deadlines, sarcasm, is formidably well read and in his spare time writes novels about Caravaggio. I wasn't quite sure why he was working there but Rowan explained that we needed him because he was the embodiment of an *ER* reader. They are typically 50 years old, well educated and the magazine represents, in the main, their only contact with anything even remotely classed as 'adult material'. Many of the 10,000 subscribers that were on the books were in their twilight years and the publication provided them with a frisson of excitement that they just didn't get from reading the *Daily Telegraph* (this was in the days before the *Telegraph* decided it wanted to be a cross between the *Daily Mail* and the *Sun* I must add).

The general lack of magazine experience within the team wasn't initially a worry as what we lacked in experience we certainly made up for in passion. Rowan had briefly worked for Ian Hislop at *Private Eye* and had then left to do a stint for *GQ* where she fell in love with the editor, her now husband Angus. Annie had done an art degree followed by various temporary assignments before stumbling across the magazine and fast tracking her way up to editorial masthead to become the magazine's deputy editor. Annie was entirely taught by Rowan. Sally had worked for American Express and then Sky TV, and had been a full-time mum for the past 18 months or so. Dea had decided not to start working for us at all as she wanted a bit more sanity and stability in her life, which was probably a polite way of saying she wanted to work for an employer that actually paid wages. Dea left almost immediately, which to Rowan was a blow but to me came as a great relief as I had no idea how I was going to pay salaries and one less at this stage was a blessing.

In the corner of the room there was a large cardboard box full of unopened mail which had started off as a small job that nobody really wanted to do and had actually become a task of such frightening proportions that everybody was in denial about it. I immediately suggested in my most upbeat come-on-team sort of way that perhaps everyone should clear their desks and tidy up the office as this was going to be a fresh start. They looked at me as if I had asked them to cut up their grandmothers into small pieces and reluctantly, and not very enthusiastically, started to shovel up piles of erotica from the floor.

A week before, Rowan had managed to secure a brilliant piece of exposure in the *Independent on Sunday* on the future of the *ER*. I had expressly asked her not to mention me in this piece as I was still at Eyestorm and had not formally handed in my notice. The article outlined a history of the magazine, which had started as a free, quarterly newsletter sent out by The Erotic Print Society to its customers. It went on to describe how the publication had grown and how Rowan and her mystery partner had purchased the magazine and now intended to relaunch it with the help of a wealthy benefactor. Rowan and I had agreed that an emphasis should be put on a continued search for funding in the hope that it would flush out a potential investor or two who might want to put up the cash for this adventure. Part of the appeal of buying this magazine was that it had a name that most people had thought they had heard of. This is probably down to people confusing it with the *Literary Review* but, whatever the reason, it always worked in our favour. In effect it was a well known brand, but one that most people had not come into contact with. Rowan had single-handedly built up exposure for this magazine by using her natural talent for promoting herself and dragging the magazine along with her. The article in the *Independent* had taken up a full double page spread and was an absolute masterpiece. Letters flooded into the office and went into the dreaded box of unopened post.

I decided I was going to tackle this job head on and started to wade through the box. I was both worried and excited about what I found. Layers of rocks can tell geologists what events have occurred back through the pages of history; the strata of mail from the last two months fitted into roughly eight categories:

1   Letters from executors of wills informing us of their clients unfortunate demise (the death of so many of our subscribers became a source of continual concern and we prayed for mild winters and the continuing effects of global warming).

2   Subscribers moving into nursing homes and therefore wanting us to change their delivery address details.

3   Letters from nursing homes insisting we stop send-
    ing the magazine as this was not the sort of material
    that they or their residents would want to read.

4   Letters stating that they had never subscribed and
    despite asking eight times we had insisted on send-
    ing this revolting little rag through their letter boxes
    and if it didn't stop they were going to call the po-
    lice/their MP/the mail-order association or break
    my legs.

5   Letters announcing that they had subscribed and
    paid (we had cashed their cheques) but that mysteri-
    ously we were not sending any magazines.

6   Unsolicited contributions for the magazine which
    tended to arrive by the cartload and seemed to be
    written by very damaged people – leaving me won-
    dering on not a few occasions whether I should con-
    tact the authorities.

7   Letters of advice on how to run a successful media
    company from people who had never run successful
    media companies.

8   Potential investors who had seen Rowan's articles
    and wanted a slice of the action for not very much
    risk.

We also had to decide where we were going to house our fledgling empire so I called a few local estate agents and started looking for a cheap little corner of Soho where we could rent a room for a pittance before the millions started to pour in. Except landlords in Soho generally don't rent their offices out for nothing and I could hear the contempt in their voice when I explained the sparse budget we had set ourselves.

I would like to be able to say that our bank balance was worryingly deficient in anything resembling working capital, but in fact we didn't even have a bank account. So we had no money to rent an office and the enormity of the task ahead of me suddenly became apparent. I had to sit down and take stock. Then within the space of a few minutes things happened that made me believe there might be some divine spirit rooting for us. Jamie Maclean, head of EPS, walked in and asked what we were going to do about renting an office. His concern was that if we left he would be lumbered with two small grotty rooms in his main offices which would be near impossible to rent out due to the nature of his business and the fact that the place was also a hell hole:

To rent: 350 square feet of a sublet office space available within niche pornographer's office. Features include a manky sofa, lots of stains, fused windows, insufficient heating in winter, no air conditioning in summer, wires hanging from the ceiling, overwhelming smell of turnips. £2000 pcm including bills.

It was not an option to rent this on the open market so Jamie kindly offered to sublet the offices to us at a very decent price. To further sweeten the deal he would also throw in the desks and computers. The price of £800 per month was agreed and we pledged the first instalment would be put through the following week. Feeling very pleased with myself after a hard day's graft I thought I would retire for the day when Rowan walked into my new office and presented me with a cheque for £1000 which was from some friends and I was not allowed to know anything more. With an office leased and a month's rent in the kitty I went home with a bounce in my stride, comforted by the thought that the wind of fortune was behind us as we sailed into the unknown.

Since this was the first company of my own I made a pledge to myself that I would always be the first in the office. I could prepare myself to be ready to attack the day, to lead the team into battle and win victory after victory. An avid fan of Genghis Khan, I would lead from the front and build an empire that stretched across the globe. The next day I arrived promptly at the office, upbeat and ready for action, with the blood of the Mongols pumping in my veins and a Starbucks latte and wholemeal muffin in my hand. As I walked in and took off my coat I noticed a man sitting on our putrid sofa in the office across the hall.

'Are you Annie?' he asked.

'Er, no.' I replied.

'Where's Annie?' he continued.

'Do you want to see some pictures of some really hairy pussies?' I had been interrupted by Mike (employed by our EPS landlord) who was compiling a 1970s retro porn book.

'No thanks, Mike.'

'How about some cunnilingus?'

'No thanks. Please. Mike!'

'Well Annie said she was going to be here at 9 a.m.', persisted the man on the sofa.

This exchange was causing a significant deflation in my mood as dreams of global domination evaporated, and I wondered what Genghis would have done in such a situation. Unable to cleave this gentleman's skull and ravage his womenfolk I decided to call Annie on her mobile to see if she was on her way. Perhaps we could all move on and I would not have to interact further with this irritating fellow who, for reasons I could not yet fathom, seemed not quite the ticket.

Annie answered the phone in a very hungover husky state. 'Oh fuck, it's the work experience bloke I said I would interview!'

'Where are you exactly?' I enquired.

'In, er, bed. A bit of a hard night at the Academy, we were having an, erm, editorial meeting', she lied feebly. 'Can you put him on so I can talk to him?'

'She wants to talk to you,' I said, my warlord gusto replaced by a feeling of being slightly hopeless and a little embarrassed about the level of professionalism being shown by one of our key employees. I offered the phone to him.

In the next few seconds everything slotted into place. As the man raised himself out of the sofa to make it to the desk on which sat the phone I noticed his cane. At the very moment that my brain pieced together the facts and deduced that this man was blind his foot connected with a box of porn films and fruit lying on the floor and he fell head first into a bin. I helped him up and handed him the phone where he continued his conversation.

'Yes, uhum, yep, OK, right, next Thursday then. Er, will you turn up this time or … oh good, yes then, bye.'

I walked the man to the lift apologizing, and generally trying to ignore the fact that he had small pieces of old sandwich stuck in his hair.

I phoned Annie as soon as I was back at my desk.

'Annie, please don't do that to me again. I don't mind lateness occasionally but standing up blind people is shocking,' I ranted.

'Blind? What are you talking about? He was coming for a proof reading job!'

I urgently needed to get my head around this publishing malarkey. I read everything I could get my hands on. The UK magazine industry is dominated by a small number of large corporations who, in turn, are owned by even larger corporations. There are a few mavericks like my personal hero Richard Desmond who made his initial money from music magazines, then from top-shelf titles and now publishes *OK* magazine and the *Daily Express* and *Star*. There is also the legendary Felix Dennis who saw a Bruce Lee film, started out publishing kung fu magazines and now presides over a business worth millions, producing magazines all over the world. There are a few single title companies – such as *Private Eye* – which have such a strong brand that they are able to stand alone, but in the main the best way to run a magazine publishing company is to spread your overheads across several titles. Being on your own was going to be hard and I knew that in the long term if I was going to take over the world I would need to make enough money to go out and buy some more titles.

The world would have to wait, however, because a more pressing problem was the complete absence of operating capital. So we started looking at fund-raising options. We had opened an account with Barclays Bank in Soho Square who claimed to be media specialists. To those thinking of starting a business I would like to expose a myth. Banks are not run by people. You may see them walking around in the branches but they have absolutely no connection to the internal workings of the company. Humans are employed in banks for marketing and appearance purposes only – to make the rest of us think that we are still in charge. These days your bank is actually managed and run by a large computer, a central brain that makes all the decisions. Whatever you ask for is fed into this computer and a complex programme works out the response based on a risk assessment. If you are a small, newly formed company the computer is automatically programmed to say no to everything you ask for. Clearly the bank weren't going to lend us any money and we were both fairly heavily mortgaged so there was a limit to putting up our own cash. There were really only two options available to us to fund the business at this stage.

First was to find a wealthy benefactor who liked the ego-enhancing idea of owning a chunk of the *Erotic Review*. The second was to tap all our mates for £5000 and try to launch with a minimum of cash.

Various friends and family had pledged money but both Rowan and I were uncomfortable with this option, not because of failure, but because we knew it would be very annoying having 30 small investors all chipping in with their ideas. As business manager I would probably spend half my time managing them or avoiding them and this didn't seem like an attractive proposition. So we decided on option two, which was to seek out potential equity investors, who would give us money in return for a share of the business. There was a ready supply of these investors who had been in contact after the big article in the *Independent* and we started to contact them.

The first meeting was with a potential investor who happened to be a subscriber thinking he could pick up the publication on the cheap. He was instantly dislikeable and was known affectionately as Robert the C**t. I never actually knew his surname as shortly after our first meeting he called Rowan and suggested that the first thing she should do was to lose me and go into partnership with him. We never spoke to him again.

Our second presentation went little better. The investor in question was not out to shaft us, but it did become clear that we needed to sharpen our act up a bit.

Investor: 'So, how much money do you need?'

Me: 'Hmmm, er.'

Investor: 'How much of the business do you want to keep?'

Me: 'Er, how much of the business?'

Investor: 'What do you think you're going to turn over in the first year?'

Me: 'Er, hmm, let's see … 5, 10 …'

Rowan: 'Look it's a brilliant magazine, lots of people love it and we just know we can make it work!'

Investor: 'What's the exit strategy?'

Rowan: 'Exit? We're going to do this for ever!'

It was clear that revved up fiery enthusiasm alone was not going to be enough to make your average tycoon part with a large wedge of cash, particularly as we didn't even know how much we needed. It was time to start growing up a little bit so I did what I always do in this sort of situation and rang my dad.

He patiently explained to me that what an investor needs to know is how much you need, what you're going to spend it on, how quickly you're going to spend it and most importantly what he's going to make and when he can get his hands on it, or the exit. To do this you needed to write a business plan which laid out your ideas and showed how the money was going to be spent.

So I locked myself in my office with a spreadsheet programme and started to plot at the top where we could expect to generate revenue. Underneath I tried to forecast what our costs would be. I then split this up into 36 columns to account for the next three years. If you subcontract the costs from the income you end up with a profit and loss per month for the next three years. Add these all together and you'll know how much money you're going to need to get going. Obviously it is more complex than this as some months you will spend more and others less, plus your revenue streams will hopefully grow over time. However, this basic outline should give a picture of what the business needs. Then you can start to change each month to forecast changes in trading throughout the year. For example, with our business we would expect to load our marketing spend around Valentine's Day in the spring and then gear it up again in September to hit the Christmas market. This spreadsheet gave me a general idea as to how much was needed and how much we could make over the next three years. When my basic template was in place I called a meeting with Rowan and Sally to go through the plan and we agreed to control our costs by sticking to a budget for the next year. The office was not really the place to do proper detailed financial projections, so I suggested we meet up at Sally's house where we could spend an afternoon summing up our ideas and agreeing the numbers. As we sat down in Sally's dining room she made an announcement.

'Before we go any further I need to tell you something. I'm pregnant.'

This was starting to become a recurring theme in my life.

'I'm due in early July,' she continued.

The same time as our pending arrival, almost to the week. Within a split second I had to decide how I felt about this. The reality was that two of the management team, the ones who actually ran the company, were going to be off with new babies at the same time when our business was at its most vulnerable. However, normal rules did not apply here. We had all taken a chance on this business and I felt a real kindred spirit with these two people.

'Well that's great news,' I said. 'I've got a little secret too.'

With the baby stuff squared off we all put our heads together and created the first draft of our business plan.

We decided that the relaunch was going to take place in February 2002 with an early publication of the March edition. Rowan had reawakened all the writers and illustrators and was working with Will, our new freelance designer, on a design which would herald a new beginning. Christmas was now around the corner and we managed to scrape enough money together to pay Annie. The rest of us made do with not getting paid anything.

It was at this time that we met two men called Mark. Again their full names escape me but they were fondly known to us as Nice Mark and Evil Mark. The Marks had made a fortune out of telecoms and, still in their late thirties, had pocketed several million each from the recent sale of their business. They were casting around for new ventures and had seen Rowan's article in the *Independent*. Evil Mark had called Rowan and a meeting was duly arranged with him the following day. I'm sure he wasn't really evil but he was clearly a very switched-on businessman, which put Rowan and I on the back foot a little. We went through all the aspects of what we were trying to do and I could tell that the business intrigued him. He thought our numbers needed a little work and so the next day he sent his accountant to spend an afternoon with me. We crunched numbers in a way that I had never seen before and were able to run several different forecasts based on varying factors. The accountant duly went back to Evil Mark and a meeting was called for the following Monday. We avoided taking them to the Academy so as to look professional. Instead, we took them to the local kebab shop.

'We like what you're trying to do,' said Nice Mark, in a very caring sort of way.

'But we want to see some commitment from you,' said Evil Mark, in a brusque matter-of-fact, evil kind of way.

'Well we've given up everything to do this,' said Rowan.

'We want to see £25,000 from each of you before we consider putting up the money,' replied Evil Mark.

This cut us dead. I had just come through the dotcom boom where people were chucking money at anything that had even the remotest online application and here we were having to divvy up £75,000. Aside from this, I wondered to myself why we needed anyone else if we were to put up that kind of money.

'If you can put up this then we will put up the remaining £200,000 that you need and we will want 40 per cent of the business,' Evil Mark continued.

Sally had gone visibly pale.

'I think we need some time to discuss this, can we come back to you tomorrow?' I concluded.

After the meeting the three of us went and had a drink to discuss what we were going to do. Sally was mortgaged to the hilt and not working and was reluctant to put in the money. I had some equity in my house and with the interest rates as low as they were I knew I could probably afford to release the £25,000 required. Rowan was in a similar position to me and we decided that we would go back with a £50,000 offer, where Rowan and I would be the shareholders. The next morning Sally had managed to find £5,000 to put in and we made a conference call to the Marks. It turned out that during the night they had also had some extra thoughts and decided they didn't want to proceed with the deal after all. They were going to buy a water plant in Estonia instead.

It was a crushing blow. I honestly thought that we were going to be able to start off the year with £250,000 in the bank, but instead we had Christmas around the corner and the world was about to grind to a halt for two weeks. We had a few hundred pounds left from our initial funds and things were looking very bleak. We decided to close for Christmas and start all over again in January.

It was late in the afternoon and I was getting ready to skip off early when a man dressed in a cheap beige suit stuck his head around the door of my office.

'Is this the *Erotic Review*?' he said hopefully.

I replied in the affirmative.

'I'm an artist. I called in to talk to somebody about my photography, to see if you could use it in your magazine,' he continued.

Annie looked after illustrations and photography but had left for the year so things were not looking good for the photographer.

'Only I've come all the way up from Sussex,' he pleaded.

'Of course we'll have a look,' I said, not wanting to turn him away after his long trip, even though he had not bothered making an appointment, which would have seemed entirely sensible given the distance he had come. 'Come in and sit down.'

'Well, basically I specialize in close up photography,' he continued, rummaging around a large art portfolio case. 'This sort of thing …'

With that he pulled out a large photo, in vivid yellow negative, of a closely photographed erect penis.

'Hmmm.'

'What do you think?'

'Nice,' I lied.

'And this is another one just before penetration,' he said, displaying an even larger print, with (presumably) the same proud phallus just about enter a vagina but this time coloured in bright green.

'Yessss,' I said, scratching non-existent goatee, in my best art appreciation tone.

'And this is the blow job one.' He was getting excited now, hitting his stride and bringing them out in quick succession.

'So tell me,' I enquired, 'do the models you use for these mind you getting up so close?'

'Oh no, I don't use models,' he explained. 'This is me and the missus.'

I dropped the picture I was holding (of his wife's tongue tip touching the throbbing purple head of HIS penis) onto the table as sure as if I had been holding his manhood myself. I had just experienced a desperately disappointing morning and all I wanted to do was get home to my pregnant wife and enjoy Christmas. Instead I was looking at dire, thinly disguised pornography which amounted to a man photographing himself, up close, screwing his old lady.

'Probably the best thing to do now is leave us a sample and I'll ask the girls to call you when they get back in January', I suggested.

I was uneasy through the whole of Christmas. I felt continually on edge and all I really wanted to do was get into that office on 5 January and get going. One thought kept going through my mind, if we had been prepared to raise £55,000 between us for the Marks, why didn't we do it for ourselves anyway and then find investment after we had launched. It seemed that if we waited until we secured full funding then it could be months, maybe even a year of not publishing. It was a critical time and our brand was at risk of vanishing completely if we didn't get it back into the market. We all needed to earn some money and my worry was that the whole thing would fall apart if we didn't take the risk and launch in February. Additionally, and crucially, Valentine's Day, the third biggest consumer event in Britain, falls in February and Sally and I really wanted the magazine launch to coincide with this to give a tail wind to our marketing spend.

I spoke to Rowan and Sally over Christmas and we all agreed that we needed to launch in February or we would not even have left the pavilion. So, on 5 January, the *Erotic Review* finally came back to life. Fifty-five thousand pounds was deposited in the bank account and we were in business.

The *Erotic Review* is a subscription magazine. Most UK magazines are sold via the news-stand but this is a very traditional and regimented market. The style and feel of the *Erotic Review* is similar to *Private Eye* or the *Spectator*, yet because of its adult content magazine retailers will simply put it on the top shelf. Now, at risk of sounding a trifle snobbish, your average top-shelf customer does not purchase publications for their literary style and flair. I would even go so far as to say that I doubt that many top-shelf customers even read one word of text in titles such as *Asian Babes* or *Horny Housewives*. Our slightly elitist, literary magazine would not have sold a single copy on a newsagent's top shelf, so we thought the best way to market this magazine was directly to the public by way of an annual subscription.

We split the running of the business in three ways. Sally was in charge of marketing and subscription management, Rowan was in charge of the actual content of the magazine and PR and I was to run production, advertising, finance and all the other general managing stuff that a managing director should do.

Rowan had mobilized her editorial team who were hard at work getting the magazine ready. They had decided to make the content more exciting by getting a journalist to write a real-life story rather than the usual fictional material. The first of these assignments involved sending one of our reporters off to an exclusive brothel in London's West End. The journalist in question, clearly the most talented and enthusiastic amongst the troupe, went by the name of The Major. He wrote a blow by blow account of his experience at the hands of a beautiful Russian woman who entertained him for an entire afternoon. And so, in early January, I received my first invoice, which I paid using cheque number 000001. The invoice was from The Major for the princely sum of two hundred pounds for: 'Expenses incurred during the writing of Posh Brothel column.' Knowing our perilous financial state he did not actually charge for his words.

Sally had put together a marketing campaign which would make our meagre cash reserves go as far as possible. The key was to spend as little as possible to attract as many customers as possible who would spend £25 for a year's subscription. By dividing your marketing spend by the amount of customers obtained you get a cost for acquiring each customer. So if you spend £10,000 on advertising and get 1000 customers your cost per acquisition is £10 per customer. If each of those customers were to pay £25 then the campaign would yield £25,000. If our cost per acquisition exceeded £25 we would run out of money very quickly indeed. Sally spent a tense week negotiating with *The Times*, *Independent*, *Telegraph*, *Private Eye* and a host of other titles. We purposefully concentrated on placing small adverts in publications which were read by our kind of customer. Since we had no credit history we had to pay for all the advertising up front and the bank balance quickly began to diminish.

I was preoccupied with advertising revenue. Unlike most start-up magazines we were a relaunch which meant that we had an existing circulation of 10,000 people, all of whom had paid a £25 subscription. This meant that we could go to advertisers and provide them with access to a very desirable market, namely horny old men with money. We had inherited a sales house whose job was to go out and obtain advertising on our behalf for a commission but it was run by a man so disagreeable that everybody in the office avoided talking to him. As a result he had no dialogue at all with the editorial staff and booked some of the most revolting advertising imaginable. In the last magazine before I became involved there was an advert for a terrifying 18-inch stainless steel dildo. The sales guys just did not get that our readers (the 50-year-old professionals remember) were never going to buy this sort of device and would actually be turned off the magazine if we continued to promote products which would be better suited to a hardware catalogue. In turn, the sales house was frustrated because magazine deadlines were totally ignored. They cited an instance two years previously where they had worked hard on getting in advertising for a Christmas issue which finally appeared in February. The result was many, very cross advertisers who refused to pay.

Rowan walked into my office a few days later and said, 'Gavin, I think we need God on our side.'

'What on earth are you talking about?'

London is an amazing city. You can walk up a street a hundred times and never notice that you routinely pass within feet of a huge, beautiful magnificent church. Rowan led me down the road to All Saints, an imposing church on the corner of Maddox Street and Mill Street which leads onto Savile Row. Inside, away from the hustle and bustle of the West End, the tranquillity of the space is breathtaking. I had taken the last £20 from petty cash, which I put straight into the donations box.

'That should do it,' I said.

'Don't think it works like that,' Rowan replied.

I prayed to God that afternoon to help us with funding for our erotic magazine or, at the very least, that he would provide us with support in other ways, like continued positive PR. Or perhaps some TV exposure.

I also said a little side prayer to Saint Juan de Dios, the patron saint of publishers (who curiously shares his holy patronage amongst alcoholics, heart patients and firefighters).

God sent us Pauline.

CHAPTER THREE

The *Erotic Review* saddles up and rides again

Ever since I first arrived in London aged 20 I had always dreamed of running my own business. I even know where my ideal office would be located. If you look south over the River Thames from Blackfriars Bridge you will see an imposing building called Sea Containers House and, perched in the centre of the top floor, is an office with the most vast window directly looking over the river. I can only imagine that it must be the best view in the city. When I first started working in London in the early 90s I would drive past my dream office in the morning and imagine having a devastatingly attractive and efficient secretary who would arrange my bulging diary, making sure my hectic and highly successful life went without a hitch. Meanwhile I would control my empire while smoking cigars and watching lots of river traffic.

The reality was somewhat different. We were sub-leasing part of a sub-let in a grotty, dimly lit corner of a pornographic book publisher's office. There was a dead pigeon trapped on the window sill directly outside my little room. The windows were nailed shut so it was impossible to move the irritating little corpse without hiring a crane and closing Regent Street, which would have possibly been excessive given the problem. The pigeon had spent a couple of seasons on the sill and had decomposed as much as it intended to. Despite the winter gales it defiantly remained firmly welded in place. Directly facing my window was a sheer windowless grey wall which blocked most of the natural light and dropped down to ground level to become part of the outside yard of the basement Thai restaurant. A continual aroma of fish oil permeated through the leaky nailed-shut windows. To the right of the wall was a balcony of a small but very posh hotel. The first day I took up occupancy I saw the TV documentary maker Louis Theroux drinking a glass of wine with some friends and was buoyed by the prospect of an endless parade of quirky-yet-faux-earnest BBC minor celebrities outside my own window. I never saw a living soul there again. Inside the office things were not much better. I had a borrowed desk held together with gaffer tape and a chair that simply fell apart whenever it felt like it. The office was split further into a large room which overlooked Liberty's on Regent Street and this is where the editorial department lived out their squalid existence (with the exception of the little corner where Chris was stationed). There was another, smaller office, not more than a cupboard really, where Rowan did her writing. It had a foldaway mattress and Rowan would spend at least two nights a week there when she was writing her column for the *Independent on Sunday*. At first I found it unusual that it took two days to write an article but in time I got used to walking into the office on a Wednesday morning to see Rowan, 36 hours into a column, bleary-eyed and with a deadline looming. I don't think she ever missed a deadline for the *Independent* and delivered her pieces handcrafted, perfectly edited and ready for press. Half the room had been turned into a wardrobe and the rest was filled with correspondence and bottles of expensive single malt whisky. The whole office was about as far away from my dream workplace as you could get, but I comforted myself with the belief that the guy in the office overlooking the Thames had probably started out like this and worked his way up to the great secretary, cigars and view. What the guy with the view probably never did, however, was deal with the post. In my previous jobs I had never given a moment's thought as to how the post makes its way from out-tray to post office box. Now I knew as I was the one doing it most of the time. Secondly, I bet he wasn't continually interrupted by having to answer questions from irate readers complaining that they hadn't had a magazine for six months and could they have a refund. I very much doubt he would have had to deal with the heavy breathing types who would ring up and ask for spanking videos. I had never even heard about these before but there seemed to be a disproportionately large section of our subscribers who wanted to know where they could get such videos. Many of the readers would ring up the office in much the same way that you might ring up a friend to ask some advice. I would love to have sold them spanking videos except it's illegal to in this country. I'll come on to that a bit later on.

Anyway, I felt more like office junior than managing director and I needed a bit of admin support, but this was going to be a difficult problem to solve on account of our rather dire fiscal predicament. Before you go into business yourself you see companies operating, even the one you worked in, and you don't give a single thought as to how they afford to pay for staff. It's a fact that the biggest single monthly outgoing for most companies is nearly always the payroll. When you set up, you imagine that you will employ people for all sorts of activities but when you are in the hiring seat you must face facts and try, where possible, to employ people who will actually bring money into the business. Anybody who doesn't bring in cash is a cost that needs to be paid for. It sounds straightforward but many people forget this basic principal. So, hiring a dogsbody was off the list and my mailboy/MD double life looked set to continue for the foreseeable future. That is, until *she* arrived.

Pauline walked in off the street and into my life. Or she may have materialized right there in the office. We shall never know. In her mid-forties she had a pretty, happy, smiling face framed by long black hair, a great figure and was clearly mad. She had a strong Canadian accent and a huge, near-hysterical, grin that went from ear to ear. She had a look of permanent wide-eyed excitement and held eye contact for a nanosecond longer than is acceptable to an Englishman. When she spoke to anyone she faced them square on, and eyeball to eyeball, making them know they were the only person in the world that existed for her at that moment in time. Pauline was, in short, an angel, a force of pure good in a world of mostly rather bad.

'Hi, my name is Pauline, who are you?' Hand out, brisk firm shake, lots of eye contact.

'I'm Gavin, the MD.'

'Oooh, you're important then.' Hand gently on my arm, eye contact excruciating, grin firmly fixed in place.

'Erm, yes, yes, I suppose so.'

'I'm looking for a job.'

'We haven't got any money, luv,' chipped in Annie.

'Oh I don't want your money, my husband's well off. My kids are at school all day, my husband works away nine months of the year. Russia. I'm spending my days bored rigid in Ascot. I heard about your magazine on the radio and came up to town to see if I could buy one, but now I've decided I would like to work here.'

'Well, when can you start?' said Rowan.

'How about now?' And with that she removes her jacket and starts tidying up the corner of the room that will become her own.

Rowan and I looked at each other and smiled. Chris sat even more upright than he normally did and I'm sure I saw a ripple of happiness cross his face. Annie looked on suspiciously, not convinced than anyone could be so nice without wanting something.

Pauline had an interesting effect on the team. At the most basic level I got my postal problem sorted out at no extra cost and didn't have to deal with irate retired colonels in need of porn. Indeed Pauline relished taking problem phone calls and would sometimes talk for hours about spanking, the Battle of Britain, hoody culture, New Labour or whatever other topics the colonels found most irksome at that particular time. At one stage she had the whole officer rank of a navy frigate writing to her. She really was a dream come true. On a company dynamic level it altered things considerably. Pauline was a total enthusiast. She enthused about everything. She was particularly enthusiastic about whatever Chris had to say on any subject. Chris had been used to being largely ignored and when he found a very attractive middle-aged lady sitting in the next desk to him who would gasp in admiration at his every utterance he suddenly came alive. One day I came into the office and actually caught Chris smiling. Annie, on the other hand, is a northern cynic and found Pauline's effusive enthusiasm for Chris irritating to the point of distraction. It took less than 24 hours for Annie to be knocking on my office door asking if she could be moved.

'I mean they're in there talking about biplanes!' she groaned.

'Annie, you're going to have to calm down. Pauline is lovely. She even bought me an apple this morning and a bowl of muesli with yogurt. She's a good, kind person. I don't understand what the problem is.'

'She's up to something. I can't believe you're falling for it now. Apple! Muesli!'

'Look, just give it a few more days.' I wasn't about to lose my new (free) post person/irate subscriber-pacifier so easily. In keeping with her mysterious ways Pauline did not appear to have a home. She was there with an enthusiastic greeting when I arrived in the morning and always bid me a farewell at the day's end. No matter how early I tried to get in she was always there, waiting, smiling and generally trying to look after me by offering to get breakfast. My guardian angel.

The first issue was by now slowly taking shape. We had commissioned a painting for the front cover which resembled the launch of a classic 1920s luxury liner except it had a few erotic twists. If you looked closely you could see the lovers bidding a fond farewell on the quayside actually had their hands down each other's trousers – it was brilliantly done. When you turned the page you saw a cut through section of the ship at sea with all the passengers engaged in numerous unspeakable acts of debauchery.

In order to beef up the content and try to appeal to a younger market we had decided that we were going to start doing a regular sex toy page, where we would get our writers to review the latest sex gadget on the market. I had by coincidence been sent some promotional literature from a sex toy distributor and decided that rather than pay retail prices we might be able to obtain a gadget for free since we were in the business. It turns out that the enterprise in question was actually run by a Welsh fireman who, when not busy extinguishing blazes in the Rhondda, had set up a sex toy wholesaler in an industrial estate in Pontypridd. He was rather predictably called Dai.

Try to picture this exchange made with what I imagined to be a burly, Welsh fireman.

'So you want free sex toys, is it?'

'Well yes, we want to review them.'

'Righto, a sort of try before you buy, is it?'

'Sort of.'

'Well, you'll be wanting the Chasey Lain Delux Signature Pussy then. Modelled on a real fanny, it is. Bloody brilliant, it is. I'll put it in the post.'

True to his word, two days later a sizeable block of pink latex arrived in the morning post. I learnt that Chasey Lain is a famous American porn actress and the device was modelled from a cast of her most intimate parts. It was very realistic and the girls informed me that it appeared to be gynaecologically correct to the finest detail. On the underside of the device there was a hole in which you inserted a battery operated multispeed electric motor called the 'Love Bullet'. When activated it shuddered and wobbled on the desk, its mass making the whole world appear to vibrate like some sort of 1970s *Doctor Who* villain. It was about as far away from real sex as you could imagine and I just couldn't get the picture out of my mind of a desperate, sad owner inserting himself into this trembling hunk of latex in a badly-lit shed in Surrey. One of our writers boxed it up and took it home to complete the bench test. His review was perfectly summarized when he stated that 'it does work, but it's rather like having sex with a couple of pounds of minced pork'.

It was all well and good getting the magazine underway but by far the most pressing thing was finding new customers. Readers paying their annual subscription were going to be our main source of income and we needed to get some in fast. To do this Sally was hard at work negotiating rates and placing adverts in all the relevant publications we had thought would be read by our target customer. We concentrated on the Sunday press as people tend to spend longer reading the papers on a Sunday. We also took out cheaper classified advertising in the back of publications rather than spend vast fortunes on display advertising in the main section of the papers. We thought that if we placed adverts near the stairlifts and wheelchair sections then we would be ideally placed to attract the attention of our desired reader. We had asked Will, our designer, to create a simple advert based on a line drawing of a voluptuous pair of breasts bursting out of a lacy bra. Underneath we put catchy phrases like 'we're giving it away free' or 'buy the Valentine gift that just keeps on giving'. The campaign would hit the street the following Sunday.

Now, after my experiences in the dotcom industry, I made a conscious decision that I was not going to employ lots of staff. They're costly, time consuming and have a tendency to complain, call in sick and go on holiday. I tried to outsource as much of the business as was possible. This has a number of advantages, the most obvious being that the less staff you have, the less looking after them you need to do. Also by outsourcing to a professional you get a better service because they are supposedly specialist in that particular discipline. Another good reason is that it helps you manage your money, which is business-speak for saying it helps you hold *onto* your money. New businesses suck up cash and sometimes you have to duck and dodge to get by. I operate simply on the basis that money is better in my account than in anyone else's, so I always tend to pay at the last minute. 'Always pay … on the court steps' was a motto I heard mentioned earlier on in my career and one that I embraced wholeheartedly. But the one bill you can never pay late is the salary cheque. If you pay your staff late they tend to take a disliking to you and start looking in the *Guardian* Media section for a new job and before you know it you're all alone in an office filled with pornography. However, if you have outsourced a particular function, if you're a few weeks late paying the invoice it's not the end of the world.

So we decided to outsource all of our customer orders to a mailing house in Sevenoaks where they were broadminded enough to handle our type of magazine and deal with our type of semi-senile, upper-class client. I gave our all-female team of account operatives free vibrators to welcome them to the family. All the details on the newspaper adverts pointed the customer directly to the mailing house and they would answer the phone 'Good morning, the *Erotic Review*' which meant we didn't have to hire customer service staff. They would deal with the orders when they came in and the cheques and credit card slips would be banked at our local branch. We had not asked our bank for any help when we launched because we knew that the central brain doesn't like to help new companies because they represent a risk, and risks don't make billions of pounds in profit. But now we needed a credit card facility and the only place we could get this was from the bank. The Barclays drone assured us that this would not be a problem and the credit card account would be ready in time for the launch.

Continuing on my outsourcing theme we had decided to retain the services of the inherited sales house. This company was responsible for selling adverts in our magazine and earned a healthy commission for every sale they made. I had to get over the communication breakdown which had resulted them in booking advertising for steel dildos and the like. As I mentioned before, the sales house was run by a man that some might call dislikeable. He was an unusual character in that he didn't seem to have any respect for anyone. In some ways you had to respect him for that. We were never quite sure what he did but fortunately he had a side-kick called Dave who, after about twenty minutes, I established undertook a great deal of the work. I decided that we would give them a six-month trial and we would try to work with them to build up our advertiser base. We met to discuss our new strategy.

Gavin: 'So we've decided we're going upmarket and we're no longer going to carry any crude or tacky advertising.'

Sales guy: 'So what about spanking videos then?'

Gavin: 'Do you think spanking video adverts are crude or not?'

Sales guy: 'Erm, yes.'

Gavin: 'Right, you've got the idea. We all now understand the new advertising strategy – think upmarket, think class, think lifestyle.'

Sales guy: 'Does that mean I am going to have to cancel the penile electrode adverts then?'

It was going to be an uphill struggle, but with a firm hand and lots of encouragement they – or rather Dave – worked hard and for the first issue attracted a healthy range of advertisers in our classified section. I wasn't sure about the legality of accepting adverts from brothels or from overseas Viagra operations but we were desperate for cash so I made an executive decision and turned a blind eye to these. It wasn't quite the look we were going for but we were heading in the right direction. To raise our advertiser profile we also gave away free full page adverts to Coco De Mer (posh sex toys), Agent Provocateur (posh knickers) and, curiously, Skoda (crap cars).

On Monday we did a final check to make sure everything was in place and the only outstanding issue was the credit card facility. Our Bank drone continued to tell us that it was all fine and that central brain had confirmed that the facility would be ready by the end of the week. This was crucial as nearly 75 per cent of our orders would be paid for by credit card. Two days before our advertising campaign went live I received a standard rejection letter from Barclays central computer informing us that they would not be offering us a credit card facility. I was incredulous. I shook in a combination of rage at the bank's lack of help and fear that our company would not make it past its first week. When I spoke to my bank drone he told me that we had been rejected because we were a new company and were considered a risk. If I cared to put my house up as collateral then the bank would be happy to extend the facility. My house became a recurring conversation with our so-called media specialist bank.

I now had a serious problem on my hands. Ten grand, about one fifth of our entire cash reserve, had been spent on a promotion that we could not collect money from. As if getting customers wasn't going to be hard enough, now we had to contend with the possibility of having to turn away their money. It was a potentially fatal blow. It takes about two months to get approval for a credit card and there was no way we could approach a new provider and get them on board by Monday morning. There was nobody to turn to. In sheer panic I called Sally to see if we could pull the adverts but because we were so late we were told that we would have to pay for the space anyway, even if they didn't run.

In despair I called the mailing house to see if they could assist. Mercifully they came up with a plan to use their merchant account for an interim period whilst we sorted out our problem. They would have to charge us a whopping 6% of the transaction value to make this happen which was way above the bank rate but I had very little option.

By Friday the magazines were printed and ready and they were posted out to the existing subscribers. That weekend I bought copies of all the papers carrying our advert and on Monday morning I got into the office excited and anxious. The whole team waited behind me nervously as I called the mailing house to see what the response had been.

We had five orders. This looked like failure on a catastrophic level. We would expect postal orders to come a few days later but we had also expected the phone orders to be coming through thick and fast. This was about as far away from thick and fast you could get. Putting on a brave face to the rest of the team Sally and I went for a walk to the coffee shop down in the street below. Sally looked pale and held her head in her hands. I must have looked the same and we desperately tried to lift each other's spirits. There really was nothing we could do but wait to see what the rest of the week bought.

Monday closed on 25 orders. Tuesday morning bought another 25 in the post and a further 30 orders by phone. On Wednesday there were 75 in the post and the mailing house was having to divert staff to man the *Erotic Review* phonelines. By the end of the week we had over 500 orders. There was a realistic chance that we might reach our target of 1000 orders.

By now the phone lines were ringing in the office. Most of the subscribers were thrilled that after a six month wait the magazine was up and running again. Many of them called up just to say how happy they were. We had over 15 calls asking where one would go to purchase a Chasey Lain Delux Signature Pussy and even more calls from readers desperate to purchase *Debbie Does Dallas* or any films involving spanking.

The BBC called and said that they had heard about our re-launch and wanted to explore the possibility of filming our organization for their series entitled *Trouble at the Top*.

Although we were not developing the magazine on the news-stand we had managed to strike a deal with Waterstone's and Borders to take our stock. Since neither had an adult section we were able to avoid the top shelf and so increased our likelihood of selling to the sort of reader who would appreciate us. Later that week I went into Borders on Oxford Street and found a pile of our magazine tucked behind *Architecture Today*. I surreptitiously swapped around the piles so that the *Erotic Review* stood proudly at the front of the rack. I then took a copy up to the payment point and purchased a copy of my own magazine. It was a moment of immense pride. By the end of week two we had reached over 1000 new subscribers and Rowan, Sally and I really started to believe for the first time that this might actually work.

A few days later the BBC turned up. *Trouble at the Top* is a successful series of programmes which follow the fortunes of companies that, for various reasons, are facing challenging times. They had liked the story about Rowan and I buying out this magazine and thought that it might fit well with their series. We sat in our grotty offices and went through our plans, objectives and what we hoped to achieve in the next twelve months. After they had gone I expressed reservations about appearing in this show. Firstly, it was going to be a tough year if we were going to make this venture work and I wasn't sure that we really needed a film crew following us around. Secondly, and on a personal level I wasn't sure I really wanted to be on television. I was in this for the money and the thrill of running a business and not to get my face all over the television. Sally, like me with a young family, just wanted to get on with the job. Rowan was keen to do it and argued that the publicity would be good for the magazine. Rowan loves being on television and is very good on screen; I was simply worried that I would look like an arse. We continued to discuss it over the next few days until the BBC team called again to inform us that they didn't think we would work. I was relieved to find out that their impression of us was that we all got on too well (so no personality clashes or big rows) and that our business plan was too organized (so no threat of imminent bankruptcy). If only they had waited six months they would have seen how wrong they were.

Our relaunch reawakened the amateur erotic writers who flooded the office with unsolicited material. All the correspondence went into the box to be dealt with at a later date. Nearly all the material was unusable but occasionally you would get a good piece and we did commission rare items from this stock pile. Some of it was so shockingly awful that it was very funny indeed. One writer had sent us a short story which was so bad we came close to publishing it. In the story a woman had hired two gardeners, strapping types who sweated as they humped around logs on her patio. While cooking in the kitchen one of them came in the house and after a brief and highly unconvincing exchange had inserted himself and the two went at it hammer and tongs standing right there in the kitchen. Before she knew it his partner had joined the action and had taken her roughly via the tradesman's entrance. This led to the most memorable erotic fiction line we had ever received: 'My bum vibrated with orgasm!'

Hardcore pornography had become more accessible in the UK over the past few years after a change in government laws made it legal to show penetration. Prior to that the only way you could see all the rude bits was to buy illegally under the counter. New 'R18' films replaced the tamer '18' films which always frustratingly managed to position a flowerpot with begonia in full bloom right in front of where the action was taking place. The films are very formulaic and it was clear that most of the writers sending us their material had seen far too many as they strictly followed the format that was in use by the industry.

Interestingly we were inundated with students looking to do work experience. Students of journalism often have a rebellious streak and you could understand how the celebrated literary magazine called the *Erotic Review* would look good on their CVs. Annie often gave them the submissions box to go through as their first job and it was not uncommon for work experience students never to return after the first day.

News of our relaunch filtered out through the media and the *Independent* sent a journalist to spend the day with us to see what it was like working in such an environment. The resultant article brought many people out of the woodwork.

Companies looking for partnerships or angles to make money started calling up, one of which had launched a new concept in pornographic websites. Their research had proven that an average male porn viewer takes four minutes to satisfy himself. Using this information they had created a website that showed four-minute film clips that could be paid for using the telephone. You called their 0990 number and listened for three minutes (at £1.50 per minute) and at the end of the call you would be given a pin number to type into the site. The beauty of this concept is that you don't have to use your credit card which means your wife doesn't find out your dirty little secret and she doesn't leave you and take the kids to her mother's. We could become part of this salubrious enterprise by teaming up with them to create our own *Erotic Review* endorsed website. At this stage I wasn't sure that we should be taking the magazine so obviously downmarket and declined the offer. In the long term we had to work towards high standards so that we could attract blue-chip lifestyle advertisers. If we didn't turn away all the low end material we would be forever in amongst the steel dildos and electric genital nodes. However it was crucial that we started to earn money from as many sources as possible so I made a decision to meet as many people in the industry as I could, to see if we could come up with a few money-spinners.

While on this enterprising streak I also decided to get into the chatline business and set up two lines to test the water. The first was called 'Posh ladies who like to chat', which was quickly followed by 'My husband's away working and I'm bored'. They are simple to set up and can be quite lucrative. I had rather naively thought that these would be sordid little operations and that you would be ringing these women at their homes where they would proceed to talk dirty to you but, as usual, I was wrong about the sex industry and things were done in a much more efficient and professional manner. I contacted the content provider and was allocated an account manager, a very switched-on graduate called Sian, who explained how it all worked.

I described what I wanted the theme of the line to be and was allocated my own 0909 number. When my client rang the number their call was routed to a call centre, which was based in a technology park in Swindon. The call centre was staffed mostly by students, out-of-work actors and part-time mums. When the call centre operatives picked up the phone a computer screen in front of them informed them of the nature of the call and they conducted the conversation accordingly.

So 'My husband's away working' line might go something like this:

Caller: 'Er, hello.'

Operative: 'Gosh, I'm so bored, my husband is away.'

Caller: 'Erm, why don't you take off your pants then?'

Operative: 'Good idea, what do you think I should do now?'

Caller: 'You could play with yourself?'

Operative: 'And I can play with you too. Gosh, you have such a big …'

And I think you probably get the idea. Rather predictably, most calls last about four minutes. The caller gets charged £1.50 per minute and 25 per cent is given to the content provider and 25 per cent is given to BT. Even though users were only using the service for an average of four minutes we were getting such a high number of callers that in the first month we made £200 from the two chatlines. Not a great deal of money but enough to pay a couple of the contributors or even take the team out for a boozy lunch

The April issue was underway and the Pauline/Annie problem had continued to get more complex. Pauline's mannerisms were making Annie so angry that she was in danger of quitting altogether and her fascination with Chris had reached a level of such overwhelming approbation that it was becoming quite a distraction. As deputy editor, Annie was in charge when Rowan was away but Pauline and Chris were not happy taking instruction from someone they saw as less experienced and half their age. An argument broke out one afternoon and the whole situation was becoming reminiscent of a playground dispute. So I sacrificed the tranquillity of my own little dim, anti feng shui-ed, dead-pigeoned space and moved Pauline into my office to work directly for me on advertising sales. It was important to have the team concentrating on generating a magazine and not indulging in small power struggles.

Now, any new business needs to look at where the money will come from. We had worked out that our two primary sources of income were going to be from subscriptions and advertising. However, I was keen to develop other revenue streams like my chatlines, and the volume of enquiries about purchasing the Chasey Lain Delux Signature Pussy made me start to think about some alternative ways of creating income. Clearly if we could start to sell stuff we could add a revenue stream onto the business which would require minimal cost. Since we already owned the magazine we wouldn't have to pay advertising costs and it occurred to me that we could start our own *Erotic Review* shop and sell products and films directly to our readers. In fact if we were clever about it we could do a good review of a product and beneath we could provide details on how the reader could purchase it.

Another of these new moneymaking ideas was to get into selling adult videos. I had been given a vintage pornographic film dating back to the mid 1920s. It was pure class. The films were different in so many ways from those of today. Firstly, the cameras used were so big that they weren't mobile enough to get close for the viewer to see what was going on. Secondly, even if they had got close up you couldn't actually see anything as the women taking part all proudly displayed pubic hair of afro proportions. The men wore tweed and kept their shoes on and the whole film played slightly too fast in the style of Harold Lloyd. Since the films were over 30 years old there were no copyright laws in force and I could copy them as many times as I liked. Fortunately, before I embarked on this copying spree, I had a meeting with a video wholesaler who informed me that what I was about to do would send me to prison on a number of counts. Firstly, the films needed to be certified, which they weren't. Then, having got them certified I needed a licence to sell them, which I didn't have (and which, in Westminster, would cost something in the region of £30,000). This caused our video enterprise to fail before we had even sold one film, but it was an important lesson in how not to launch headlong into a new venture without doing the necessary groundwork. This didn't stop us venturing into the sale of sex toys and one day the Rampant Rabbit came into our lives.

The Rampant Rabbit is the best-selling vibrator in the world. It is a multifunctional, multi-speed, multicoloured masterpiece. It is a design classic, a tribute to feminism, and I have heard it said that in the not-too-distant future it will make men surplus to requirements. The Rabbit has three functions. The standard shaft which can be used without power as a simple tool of pleasure. Turn button A and a series of internal beads rotate creating an undulating surface on the shaft which is supposed to drive women wild with pleasure. The *pièce de résistance*, however, is the actually 'rabbit' appendage which rises from the lower end of the shaft at 45 degrees. This crucial piece of engineering is topped with two 'ears', hence the Rabbit name, which are designed to sit either side of the clitoris. When button B is pressed the attachment vibrates sending the user to a hitherto unvisited plane of ecstasy. The whole structure is covered in a semi fluorescent pink latex waterproof coating and smells not unlike Play-Doh. When women hold them they seem to look powerful and independent, when men hold them they seem to become meek and inadequate. When Charlotte from *Sex in the City* purchased her Rabbit she did not leave her apartment for seven days.

The Rabbit was sent to our bench-testing panel who concluded that the device delivered a jaw juddering climax and was indeed the Ferrari of the sex toy world. This was going to be our first item of merchandise to be sold in the *Erotic Review* shop.

While all these fun and games were taking place it became very clear, very early on that our £55,000 was not going to go very far. Once the wage bill, rent, postage, printing and contributors were paid the bank balance was looking decidedly unhealthy. Also we had taken on £30,000 of miscellaneous debts and these people had heard about the relaunch and were keen to get their money back. Now I had a taste for the business and we had an idea as to how the marketing would perform I calculated that we needed another £200,000 to get us to a stage where we would start to make a profit. Without investment we were going to run out of money in approximately four months.

CHAPTER FOUR

More money woes (and not very posh ladies who like to take off their clothes)

To many men of my generation there really is only one car we aspire to. A Porsche. Now there are lots of other great super sexy cars out there but to a budding entrepreneur a Porsche marks a milestone. It's a first mark of success. Ask almost any successful businessman what their first decent car was and you'll nearly always get the same reply. A Porsche. They may grow up and get a Bentley or big Mercedes or simply lose the plot altogether and get a Lamborghini. They may have inferiority issues and get a Range Rover but I bet you a fiver the Porsche is the one they remember. It's not too ostentatious, it drives like a dream, it's quick off the mark, it sounds great when you start the engine and the interior smells … like success. But the thing that appeals to us is that it nearly always represents a year's salary. You're effectively saying to the world that after years of driving crap Vauxhalls and suffering budgetary restraints where you're always watching how much fuel you put in the tank, that you are confident enough in your own ability to blow a year's worth of graft on a thing that's going to get you from A to B at 15 miles to the gallon. You're not saying you're a billionaire, you're saying 'things are going well enough for me to splash it around a bit'.

Four months into my new venture I found myself in the unfortunate position of having made no money at all. In fact, I was at a point opposite to making money. I had borrowed money to pour into a loss-making business. I was starting from a negative position and I also had a baby on the way, so a transport solution was essential otherwise I'd have to bring Katharine and baby home from hospital on the tube.

Which would be bad apparently. So a Porsche was, at this stage, a long way out of reach. Not only was there the harsh fiscal reality of not actually being able to afford one, but there was also the fact that I needed a car with a hatchback so I could get a travel cot, sterilizer, activity play mat and all the other voluminous paraphernalia that comes when an infant enters your life. So I purchased a third-hand ancient Saab hatchback, the interior of which smelt of … old shoes, and had thousands of tiny scratches on it which made me suspect it might have been used as a fleet car for a barbed wire sales executive. I had a long way to go. Dinner party scenarios were not appealing.

Other Guest: 'So what do you do Gavin?'

Gavin: 'I run a bankrupt, quite rude magazine which is aimed at retired upper-middle-class males.'

Other Guest: 'Interesting – I work for a merchant bank. So what do you drive?'

Gavin: 'Blue, 1985 Saab, scratched, very large hatchback for baby stuff (ample room for an activity play matt).'

Other guest: 'I've got a Porsche. I don't have an activity play matt, I have a nanny.'

Score: 2–0 to guest, Griffiths on the bench with a suspected fractured ego.

Dinner parties would be avoided for the time being.

By now it was March and raising investment was becoming an obsession. I was following up every lead I could to try to find some money, and nearly all were ending up in frustrating cul-de-sacs rather than sweeping avenues of opportunity.

There were two distinct kinds of people we were talking to: investors who had the money to put into the business themselves or people who could secure investment on your behalf for a fee. Beware of the latter. There is actually a very sizeable consultancy sector operating out there of people who call themselves fundraising agents. The pitch works like this.

You pay them £2000 to write you a business plan.

You then pay them a monthly retainer of around £300 to cover their expenses.

You agree that if they find an investor they take five per cent of the money raised.

Sounds good, you sign a contract.

They then do absolutely nothing.

You can see the appeal from their perspective. If they get a couple of mugs a month it makes a tidy living for not really doing anything. On very rare occasions one of these consultants will actually do the job. Ninety-five per cent of the time they will waste your time and money. If you decide to go down this road then it's imperative that they give you details of three deals they've done in the last year with names of people you can contact to get a reference. If they can't, run a mile.

There was a third type of person, probably best described as an amateur fundraiser, who is looking for a job or for something – anything – to fill their shallow little lives. It became very obvious that there were a lot of these people around who liked to talk about getting investment, but had no hope whatsoever of procuring it for us. It was as if they enjoyed the attention we gave them, and in the early days we courted them as if they were potential lovers. Rowan did lots of TV pundit work and had almost reached minor celebrity status, particularly within the *Erotic Review*'s readership bracket, so it was no coincidence that there were lots of 50-plus men queuing up to give us advice. Before we had realized they were just time wasters they would get the full treatment; the tour of Erotic Towers, complete with elevenses on the manky couch, lunch with Rowan and I in the Academy, coffee with Annie and an in-depth conversation about model aircraft with Pauline as they were escorted out to the lift. After the fifth one of these we rolled up the red carpet and decided that it would be cheaper and less annoying if I simply checked them out myself over a coffee and a muffin collected by the ever useful Pauline. The disappointment on their face when they came to the office and had to meet me was palpable. Sally called them 'star-fuckers' as all they really wanted to do was meet a TV personality. I preferred to call them fuckers. One of these was a portly, late-middle-aged man who called himself Norm@n – yes, that's right, Norm@n – who had worked in insurance or something non-erotic-magazine related and promised to help us. Actually, all he really wanted to do was hang around the office sandwiched between Annie and Pauline and sniggering at his own *double entendres* which, let's face it, when you work in an office that publishes the *Erotic Review* were fairly easy to come by. We almost had to ban him from the office as he was becoming a nuisance and I wondered what Genghis would have done under the circumstances. I heard that if he respected his enemy he would kill them in the honourable Mongol way, which was to break their back by being snapped in two over a bench and then let whatever life remained drain out of them on the freezing permafrost of the steppe. This was for people he respected. People who he thought had treacherous motives were boiled alive. Possibly one of the most painful and gruesome death sentences devised.

'Pauline, pop the cauldron on, Norm@n is coming to visit.'

I was starting to despair at how we could possibly get our funding, but as a good friend always tells me, to find your funding Prince Charming you have to kiss a lot of frogs. And then Jack Lang came into the office and indirectly ended up saving us. Although he was not a prince, nor particularly charming.

Jack is famous in technology circles and is wise and rich. He's got rich by doing good deals – at least, good deals from his perspective. He marched into my office, sat down and offered me fifty grand for half the company pretty much straight off the bat. At the time I owned 45 per cent of the business. This deal would have effectively scrunched Rowan and I down to about a 20 per cent stake each, making me a minority shareholder working for a technology baron. Hardly the dream of working for myself I had envisaged. When Rowan and I had looked at getting investment we were thinking of giving away 30 per cent so that collectively we could retain control over the destiny of the empire. This deal looked like a bit of a turkey and we very politely declined the offer.

Realizing that we weren't going to accept his unsatisfactory offer, he informed me that my business plan was crap, my numbers were a joke and that if I was ever going to make it in the business world I needed a finance person, and he was going to put me in touch with Michael Carter. Michael changed everything for me forever. He taught me about money and how to use it. It's an important lesson for any entrepreneur: when you go out on your own, try and get someone around you who knows about money because keeping books and managing accounts is boring. To be honest I'm bored writing about it, but it is so important to keep your financial records in order. It doesn't have to be a fully fledged finance director; even a reasonably attentive, part-time book keeper can keep you on the path of fiscal righteousness. I don't mean stop worrying about money.

Never stop worrying about where the money comes from or who needs to be paid. Nearly all entrepreneurs I know can tell you yesterday's sales figures to the nearest tenner and what their bank balance is. Someone has to put your income and expenditure in the right columns so you can get some accounts done, which is a legal requirement every year for as long as you run your business. Often, in the thrill of launching a business, many people lose sight of this. If you can get a financial grip from the outset it makes the job much more manageable. This is what is expected of you:

- Keep a full record of income, expenditure, assets, and liabilities. These records must be kept safe as you'll need them for doing the company's annual accounts. You should keep these detailed records for at least seven full tax years.

- Pay income tax and national insurance contributions for any employees. If you are a director and are paying yourself a salary, you are an employee of the company.

- File annual accounts at Companies House. These are available for the general public to review, if they so wish. This includes a profit and loss account, a balance sheet and, if your turnover is in excess of £5.6 million or your balance sheet totals more than £2.8 million, you will need to provide an auditor's report from a qualified auditor.

- Complete an Annual Return each year to confirm basic details relating to the company, such as directors' names and registered company address.

- Complete an annual corporation tax return and pay the amount of tax and National Insurance due within nine months of the Company year end each year.

Finally, someone with a convincingly basic level of accounting knowledge will be able to tell you if you are trading legally. If you're starting out with limited funds and sailing close to the wind you need to ensure that you are not trading insolvently. Insolvent trading is illegal and if you do it you forgo the protection given to you by your limited company.

in·sol·vent

– *adjective*

not solvent; unable to satisfy creditors or discharge liabilities, either because liabilities exceed assets or because of inability to pay debts as they mature.

Michael was sent to protect me not by whatever mysterious entity had sent Pauline but by Jack Lang and I will always thank him for introducing us. Michael is a fairy godfather, favourite uncle and devil's advocate all rolled into one. He walks everywhere so consequently always arrives at his chosen destination slightly out of breath and a bit hot. He dresses like an accountant, predominantly M&S with comfortable footwear, and sports a sixth-form haircut. He doesn't really enjoy small talk but has a go anyway, which can make conversations with him stunted and not pleasant. If you have something to say then fine, likewise if he has something to say then that's also fine. If you don't have a point or anything earth-shatteringly intriguing to convey then it's best to remain silent, which at first is awkward but once you realize that's how he likes it, it's quite pleasant. Considerable effort goes into creating small talk and it's a relief not to have to engage in it. You don't have to waste time thinking of banal things to say.

Gavin: 'So, you're going on holiday this summer?'

Michael: 'Finland.'

Gavin: 'Ooh, that sounds fun.'

Michael: 'Yes.'

Gavin: 'Er. Can you pass the salt?'

Michael: 'Yes.'

Gavin: 'Any plans for Christmas?'

Michael: 'No.'

They say that there is a fine line between madness and genius and I suspect that if I had to choose between the two,

Michael flops slightly on the genius side. It's a hair's breadth away from the former though. However, he has a knack of explaining accountancy and making it understandable, and in a very short time everything that had previously been so daunting clicked into place. He helped me make sense of the fiscal workings of a business and without doubt he is one of my favourite people in the world. I hope to enjoy many quiet lunches in the future with him, not talking. More than anything I regret not making him rich. Twice. So Michael arrives, hot, hair ruffled, out of breath and he sits in my office, looks around unfazed by the porn, pauses and says, 'Right. Let's get you some money.'

So I tell him about my ideas.

1   Friends and family investors. Ruled out because you should never do business with friends or family. Or people called Jack.

2   Big rich man who has £200k kicking about. Proving elusive.

3   Sell shares to the readers. This was my latest cunning plan. I had heard of a football club who when faced with an empty bank account sold shares to those investors they knew would be interested in their business. Their fans. What a perfect idea. They are already into the concept of the club, they already fork out £25 a game so why not sell them

a chunk of the club for £500. I thought the same thing might work for our readers. It was an expansion of my friends and family idea except they were one step removed. We had ten thousand subscribers. Most of these were men, getting on a bit, got a few bob, probably retired colonels, probably read *Shares Magazine* and would absolutely love the opportunity to acquire shares in the *Erotic Review*. Particularly if Rowan chairs the AGM. And they can get a photo of the editorial team in their nighties at Christmas.

Michael absolutely loves this third option. 'Only problem is,' he says, 'if you do it now you'll go to prison.'

Not wanting to go to prison (another close shave with incarceration in only a few weeks) I pressed him further on this point.

Curiously, it seems that you can't simply flog off shares to as many people as you like. If I wrote a prospectus outlining the benefits of owning shares in the *Erotic Review* and sent it to our 10,000 readers then I would be making a public offer. And the only companies who can make public offers for shares are PLCs and, you guessed it, we were not a Public Listed Company. I know I should have listened closer to this stuff at school. Anyway, the point is that the authorities take a rather dim view of amateurs hocking shares all over the place willy-nilly and adopt a rather tough line with anyone caught doing it. PLCs require a lot more administration and corporate governance than the regular old Ltd company, which I suppose is there to prevent charlatans setting up bogus organizations and flogging shares in South Sea bubbles and fictitious African mining companies. Anyway, the only way I was going to get my 'sell readers shares' caper off the ground was to set ourselves up as a PLC. So, thrilled at the prospect of being finance director of the *Erotic Review* PLC, Michael left the office to investigate what we had to do to get this off the ground.

One thing I found particularly difficult was to discipline myself to do quite different jobs at the same time. Raising funds is actually quite a hard job fraught with disappointment and time wasters. The flip side is that you have to keep your business going, motivate the people around you, try to make money and attempt to banish to the back of your mind the fact that you only have enough cash to keep trading until summer. In the middle of trying to set up a PLC I also embarked on one of the strangest episodes of my life. The launching of the website called Poshtotty.com.

Now the whole concept of Poshtotty.com was inspired by another website called VillageLadies.com. It was such a supremely wonderful idea that we had to have a go at doing it ourselves but with our own twist. Village Ladies inhabit a cyber village, a sort of virtual Cotswold hamlet where gardens are tended, jam is made and tea is supped. And clothes are removed. It's soft porn of a nature that we just don't see very often. Subtle, funny, slightly arousing if only because you simply never see these kind of people getting their kit off anywhere else. The ladies ranged in age from their late thirties to their early sixties and it was a complete hoot. I actually imagined that the guy who ran it got as much pleasure putting the thing together, if not more, as the sad blokes fumbling with themselves over their keyboards after parting with £25 a month.

I just had to run a site like this and with complete disregard from the practicalities of actually doing it, proceeded to launch our latest venture.

Rowan was busy with the magazine so it was agreed that I would take responsibility for the setting up and running of this new project. But how to launch a website? The only time I had ever been involved in a website launch was when we had raised $25 million and had a team of programmers, a team of web designers, a team of people who did something called 'liaison' and a person called Elizabeth who seemed to spend her whole time on a plane flying first class around the world complaining that she spent all her time on a plane flying first class around the world. If I was going to have a dotcom business how could I possibly afford to send someone full time on a plane, let alone first class? How could I afford a team of designers? What about the mojitos in New York and company credit cards? Well I couldn't afford all this so Michael taught me about dotcom lite: the new way of launching your online business without the need to talk to a venture capitalist or spend millions on a cast of thousands to run it. More boring though to be honest, because there is nothing truly more exciting than pissing a venture capitalist's cash up against the wall on hand-crushed lime and tequila cocktails at 3 a.m. in the Meatpacking District. Anyway, the secret formula for dot-com lite is that you cut everyone needed to launch the site in on the deal. You make their earnings contingent on the venture generating a profit.

So Michael introduced me to a chap who could design and build websites. He was given a percentage of the profits. I then contacted an old friend of my wife's called Roberta who owned a PR firm and she agreed to work on a percentage of future profits. Then I called on my friend Triggers O'Grady who could be counted on to take a few snaps for, you guessed it, a share of the profits. So in total we had to give away about 40 per cent of the profit of the site but we didn't have to spend any money upfront on content, web building and publicity. We probably saved about £50k worth of cost and nobody had to go on a plane. All we needed was a concept and we found it one afternoon. Rowan and I were sitting on the manky sofa discussing what we were going to call this exciting new project. I was thinking posh ladies. Had to be something posh. I liked the whole idea of posh ladies, going to Ascot, eating scones, arranging some flowers and then taking off their clothes. The key to it was not to be overtly pornographic. It had to be sexy in a way that most sites weren't. It was all going to be tasteful and fun. And by the end of the day we had the name: Poshtotty. co.uk. And so naively, and without consciously deciding I was doing it, I meandered around it and then accidentally reversed directly into it. 'It' being the real world of adult entertainment.

What I hadn't really thought about at this point was the posh ladies themselves. It was as if I had put the cart before the horse. How was I going to actually persuade a posh lady each week to take off her clothes and be photographed? I asked Rowan who was posh, Oxford educated and attractive (and therefore fit the bill to a tee) if she would be the first – naturally she looked at me as if I was insane, Annie threatened to slap me and even the ever obliging Pauline refused point blank. Had the *Erotic Review* team agreed, however, it would still have left me with another 49 posh ladies to sort out in the next year on the assumption we released a new one each week. Plus we needed a whole load of them to start off with. What was required was a critical mass of semi-nude, upper crust womanhood to give the thing some momentum, get some press coverage. I mean you could hardly launch the site with one lady and expect the punters to part with £25 a month. I started to ask all the posh ladies I knew and then the less posh until it got to a point where I was asking fairly distant acquaintances if they wouldn't mind getting their kit off for our new site. Surprisingly all said no. Why was I always getting thwarted? Genghis would have simply raided a town, put the men to the sword and had their womenfolk dress up in twin set and pearls and a nice pair of court shoes for his new site. In the absence of the ability to murder and pillage at will the only things I had in my armoury were charm and cash. Clearly the charm hadn't worked and the cash reserves were meagre – not nearly enough to hire top-end talent. I might have got Sophie Dahl (posh, famous grandfather) for five minutes which was hardly going to result in an engaging and much talked about website. I was going to have to use limited resources, wily cunning and much imagination to make this work. I bet this is what Richard Branson would have done, although he would have found a way to fit a hot air balloon in there somewhere.

So what does a man do to persuade cut-price, slightly desperate well-to-do ladies to undress on camera and appear on a website? Well after much research I found my answer: hire glamour models.

I wasn't really aware at this point that there were different types of models. I had simply thought that there were supermodels and non supermodels. I suppose if I had thought about it, it makes sense, but I can honestly say that I had never spent a moment's time thinking about the echelons of the modelling industry prior to this point. The fact that there is a model hierarchy was a revelation.

- *Catwalk, Editorial and Fashion Modelling* (modelling royalty).

- *Advertising and Commercial Modelling* (minor hanger-on royalty, think Duchess of Kent or the horse-riding one dating the rugby guy).

- *Catalogue Modelling* (middle strata, reasonable pay and unlikely ever to be asked to shove a glass dildo up their bottom).

- *Exhibition and Promotional Modelling* (the grafters of the modelling world, standing on their feet all day at car exhibitions in a tight T-shirt looking bored and dreaming in vain about that catwalk which will always elude them, but at least they can say model in their passport under the occupation bit).

- *Glamour Modelling* (they are not selling things which is what the other models do, they are selling themselves. Crucially, they don't need to have good looks, although large breasts will help. The spectrum is vast, from Page 3 stunnas, through to porn models. High probability that their career will end at the lower end of the decency spectrum. High probability someone will eventually ask if they can shove a glass dildo up their bottom).

- *Life Modelling* (hobby modelling for a bit of extra cash, 'cool' students or pensioners who feel liberated).

- *Look-a-Like Modelling* (tragic, spending your life pretending to be Posh Spice and always wearing a look of thinly veiled disappointment).

- *Plus Size Modelling* (fat people who are 'proud' of the fact they eat too many cakes and don't exercise).

- *Speciality Modelling* (not really models, someone who perhaps has nice hands).

- *Child Modelling* (the lowest of the low, an outlet for pushy parents to make up for the regret of lost opportunities).

So, glamour modelling was where I was going to start my search and, if I was lucky, I might get some acting skill so they could at least pretend to be posh. Further research revealed that the place to find glamour models/actresses in abundance was to advertise in *The Stage* newspaper. And when I started looking in *The Stage* I realized what I was doing. I was asking women to take their clothes off. I was asking women to take their clothes off so that I could photograph them and put them on a website. To make money. Oh my god. I WAS A PORNOGRAPHER. It simply had not occurred to me up to that point that I was doing anything other than having a bit of a fun and doing what was in essence an extension of the magazine. Which was certainly not porn. How had I allowed myself to do this? Why hadn't anyone stopped me?

Here are some examples of adverts that appear in *The Stage*:

- Pluto, London's premier fully nude table dancing venue. Earn £2000 a week.

- The Top Deck requires pole dancers. Cheap accommodation arranged.

- Female singer with dancing ability required – for top professional girl band.

- Karaoke host required. Must have own car and bikini. (Eh?)

But it was too late to back out. The newly formed Poshtotty team was ready to roll and the business was desperate for cash. We knew we only had a few months left before we ran out of money so I had no choice but to push on. I consoled myself with the fact that it was fairly mild soft porn and it would all be done in an arty way which might stop people from ever accusing me from being a pornographer.

And even if I was, it hadn't stopped Richard Desmond – now owner of the *Daily Express* and one of the country's richest men – from making his fortune.

So the advert was faxed over and appeared in the following week's issue of *The Stage*.

Wanted: Posh ladies to take their clothes off for a new exclusive web site. Call us now on 0207 439 8999.

They started ringing almost as soon as the newspaper was published. It was terrifying.

First caller [very harsh Essex accent]: 'Ello? Ello? Er, yes love, I'm responding to your advert for posh ladies.'

Gavin [completely out of my depth]: 'Er, yes, er hi, um, it's this site we're launching you see, we need you to, er, er, how shall I put this, er, take off your clothes and we're going to photograph you.'

First caller: 'Yes, that's fine love, will that be underwear, nude or are you looking to do spread shots, I charge extra for spreads, except not this week 'cos I'm on and I don't really like doing full frontal when I'm on, you know what I mean?'

Gavin: 'Er yes, OK, do you want to pop into the office and we'll chat about it.'

So the next day Valerie came into the office. Your cannot imagine how seedy it feels inviting someone you have never met up to the office to interview her for a site in which she is going to take her clothes off. I had figured that with the right setting and props you could make anyone look posh. Valerie proved this assumption to be very wrong. Valerie was the diametric opposite of posh and no amount of make-up was going to change that. She was anti-posh. Thin, and not thin in a good, fit, gym going, eat five pieces of fruit a day sort of way. Thin in a not very well nourished rather ill with yellow skin kind of way. Yellow peroxide hair with black roots and yellow teeth. She took off her jacket to reveal a very amateur tattoo of a big blue key at the top of her arm. Why? Why would someone choose to have a big key tattooed on their arm? Valerie brought in a suitcase on wheels clanking it against the desks and she sat on the manky sofa. All the models had suitcases on wheels. To this day whenever I see a woman walking through town with a small suitcase on wheels I imagine she's going up to an office to strip in front of some down at heel, lowlife porn director. Valerie opened her suitcase and pulled out her portfolio, I could see it was full of threadbare lingerie and a rather careworn boa. There can be nothing so tragic as a boa on its last legs.

'Sorry about the suitcase, luv,' she says, 'I'm on my way to work.'

I never found out what the work was. I did not have the courage to ask.

I flicked through the portfolio, trying to think of something to say, feeling bad for Valerie, how she must have to endure so much disappointment, to have to go through *The Stage* newspaper each week pitching up to offices and basements for crappy jobs which require her to get her kit off and get her scraggy frame out. I felt bad being part of it.

'Valerie, we've got a lot of people to see today,' I lied, 'we'll give you a shout next week if we're going to use you.' I might as well have said 'don't call us, we'll call you' and although I tried to be sincere I'm sure she could see right through me. It was a depressing experience.

The phone kept ringing with girls asking for more information and I was smart enough this time to ask them to send some pictures first to see if they would fit in with the posh theme of the site, so at least I wouldn't have to get girls in who were totally unsuitable and sit there feeling guilty. That afternoon a girl rang called Noushka who was from Gdansk. Poland had recently joined the EU and the younger more enterprising Poles had led the first wave of their great migration through Europe, many of them coming to London soon to be followed by the famous plumbers and electricians. Noushka rang from a mobile to say that she was in Soho this very minute with her friend and could she swing by and talk about the assignment. Her English was poor but the thought of bagging two posh ladies in one meeting was an opportunity I could not pass off. Besides, who was going to know if they were posh or Polish? They might even have some chums who were up for it. Hell, I could fill the whole site with pseudo posh Polish women. Noushka and Anja turned up in the office. They were both beautiful, clearly naive and both very young. I doubt they were even 18. They hauled behind them the obligatory suitcases and my heart sank. Clearly I wasn't going to employ them because although I had faced up to the fact that I was engaging in pornography I wasn't about to pass another immoral milestone and become a paedophile pornographer. It wasn't just a question of disappointing my mother or the moral issue, there was also the fact that I would go to prison and everyone would call me a nonce and do unpleasant bottom-related things in the communal shower. The fact that these two girls were putting themselves in this position was terrifying and I did my best to talk them out of following this career path. There could be no good outcome for them. Our offices were on the outskirts of Soho and I could only imagine what sort of people they were going to be seeing that day. I sat them down and in my best fatherly manner asked them what they thought they were doing. They had arrived two days ago and were dancers back home. I suggested that the best starting point for them was to work in McDonalds; it was much safer and although not great for acne it wouldn't result in a rapid descent into a life of degradation and casual violence. They both looked at me doubtfully. Not giving up so easily I rang the McDonalds head office and got the number for the recruitment hotline. I scrawled it on a piece of paper and handing it over begging them to try it while talking up the benefits of burger flipping and the sheer exhilaration that must come from making it as Ronald's employee of the month. But the duo were having none of it. They had been told that the streets of London were paved with gold and they were determined to get their share of it. They were going to be famous dancers in London and return to Poland rich and happy. I often wondered what happened to them.

The search for posh ladies for our site was clearly not going to be easy and I wondered how many of those Valerie/Noushka encounters I could take. I mean I was a nice guy, I didn't have what it took to reject all these tragic people. So

I did what any self-respecting manager would do under the circumstances. I decided to delegate. I took Pauline aside.

Gavin: 'Pauline, can you come into my office, I need to have a chat with you.'

Pauline: [walks in with huge grin] 'Sure Gavin, what can I do for you?'

Gavin: 'Pauline, I have a challenge. It's a challenge that I can only give to a trusted person.'

Pauline: 'Well, you know you can trust me.'

Gavin, speaking quickly: 'I would like you to be in charge of casting for Poshtotty.com.'

Pauline: 'I would LOVE to do that.' [untrammeled joy]

All was good with the world, equilibrium had been re-stored. Pauline had found her calling as a casting director and I didn't have to sit through any more of these dreadful soul-crushing interview sessions.

The way it would work from now on would be that I would get the applications, and all the ones that I thought might have the potential to be 'poshed up' I would pass to Pauline who would interview them. She would then weed out the mad ones, the ones on crack, or those who were children (professional portfolio shots often make girls look much older so you request a copy of the passport), then we would have ourselves a shortlist and once that was done we could get a shoot lined up.

By the third day the phone was ringing off the hook with models wanting to come and see us. Many models have their portfolios online or digitized so lots of applications were coming into my email account and I was getting dozens of photos into my inbox every day. I had always wanted something different to do but this was unbelievable. I was actually getting girls I didn't know sending me naked shots of themselves. Almost without exception they struck this slightly ditzy schoolgirl, coy, looking up from under the fringe look. It was the sort of look a five-year-old girl might have when busted stealing a toffee. Marilyn Monroe made it work, few others ever have. It is not sexy and looks remarkably stupid, and I wondered why they all did it.

I started to think there might be a low-end glamour model school where they learn this pose and are given a small wheeled suitcase, a belly button piercing and a very bad tattoo on the day they leave.

I started going through the naked photo emails and forwarding those that passed the posh test to Pauline. I was feeling guilty at first. Guilty at being married and an almost-dad and looking at naked ladies at 11 o'clock in the morning. Guilty at looking at naked ladies because I've always been guilty about stuff like that. Guilty that my mum might find out about me looking at naked ladies at work. Guilty that this didn't seem like a proper job and that I knew people at this very moment in time who were wearing suits and talking about cranes. But slowly it subsided. This was work, I was an entrepreneur and I was creating a media project that would support my beautiful spouse and our unborn child. Bit by bit it became normal and after a while it became work, and a short time after that it became boring.

Most of the girls didn't look that posh, but with the magic of the brilliant computer software called Photoshop you could work wonders. Tattoos could be removed, teeth whitened, ears tucked away and eyes brightened. Providing we had some decent building blocks and a bit of confidence we could work magic.

By the following week they were coming into the office. Pauline kept them away from me and was brilliant at explaining what we wanted. And I eventually got a real posh totty. Lavinia was from Sloane Square, was exquisitely posh, had appeared in *The Bill* (presumably as someone posh) and was 70 years old. She was going to be our first poshtotty and as a bonus she was going to bring her own vintage basque and suspenders so I didn't have to worry about finding an outfit for her. Fortunately, this encounter did make me think for the first time about what the girls would wear on the shoot and we promptly made it a condition of doing the job that you had to bring posh clothes. This not only meant I didn't have to worry too much about it but also that I was saving a bit of cash from the non-existent wardrobe budget.

By Friday we had our cast lined up and the next thing we needed to arrange was our first photo shoot.

Michael, meanwhile, had been looking at what we had to do to become a PLC. It looked like a complete pain in the arse and I rather wished I had not mentioned it.

This is what you need to set up Limited Company (Ltd):

1   One director and one company secretary

2   The ability to sign your name

3   A pound for share capital

This is what you need to form a Public Limited Company (PLC):

1   A PLC must have at least two members and at least two company directors. The secretary (or each joint secretary) must also be a person who appears to the directors to have the necessary knowledge and ability to fulfil the functions and who:

    (a) held the office of secretary or assistant or deputy secretary or
    (b) for at least three of the five years before their appointment, held the office of secretary of a non-private company; or

(c) is a barrister, advocate or solicitor called or admitted in any part of the United Kingdom; or

(d) is a person who, by virtue of his or her previous experience or membership of another body, appears to the directors to be capable of discharging the functions of secretary; or

(e) is a member of any of the following bodies:

- the Institute of Chartered Accountants in England and Wales;
- the Institute of Chartered Accountants of Scotland;
- the Institute of Chartered Accountants in Ireland;
- the Institute of Chartered Secretaries and Administrators;
- the Chartered Association of Certified Accountants;
- the Chartered Institute of Management Accountants (formerly known as the Institute of Cost and Management Accountants); or
- the Chartered Institute of Public Finance and Accountancy.

2 A PLC has only seven months after the end of its accounting reference period to deliver its accounts to the Registrar. A civil penalty will be incurred if it delivers accounts to Companies House after the statutory time allowed for filing.

3   A newly formed PLC must not begin business or exercise any borrowing powers until it has a certificate issued under section 117 of the Companies Act 1985 confirming that the company has issued share capital of at least the statutory minimum.

4   £50,000 worth of share capital (of which 25% must be purchased already).

In amongst accidentally becoming a pornographer, trying to set up a PLC and not having any money, issue three of the magazine was starting to take shape.

Our second issue, April 2002 was now out in the shops. It was the Eastern Karma Sutra edition. Most of the articles were themed in some sort of eastern way and it felt exciting that we were motoring along and cranking out an issue each month.

Work continued on the next issue of the magazine. As with the Karma Sutra issue Rowan tried to tie each magazine together with a theme, thereby avoiding the problem of just publishing filthy stories each month which might get a bit tedious. The May issue, our third issue, was going to be about Spring or something vaguely topical. However, at the last minute Rowan got invited to Paris and disappeared for the week. The guys in the office had been working on whatever the original concept was and, without direction, the good ship *ER* became utterly rudderless. Morale dropped like a stone and quite inexplicably nothing happened until she returned the following Monday. When this happened the whole office restarted, like a machine whirring back into life. Annie and Chris, who spent the last week morose and forlorn like a couple of abandoned puppies, were enthusiastic and in good cheer. With two weeks to deadline the theme of the issue changed to Paris and the team effectively started again, working through the night getting it finished. I couldn't imagine a more crazy, haphazard way of functioning. But this was a steep learning curve and it became clear that when you work with creative types the rule book goes out the window – and so long as the magazine was produced on time, who was I to complain? It was a long way from my days in the shipping industry.

Despite the chaotic working conditions that prevailed under Rowan I felt like we were making ground. Everyone knew what they were doing and from the outside we were a functioning publishing outfit, which was all that counted.

Back at home Mrs G was getting large. She had given up her much-loved job and was nesting, preparing the house for our pending arrival a few months down the road. Katharine's parents had come to help us complete the renovations we had started but hadn't really got round to finishing. The countdown to late June now began in earnest.

Late June: Griffiths Jr due

Late June: *Erotic Review* runs out of cash

We really had to find some money and lady luck was about
to smile on us.

CHAPTER FIVE

Three knights in shining armour and a suitcase full of cash

'Entrepreneurs are simply those who understand that there is little difference between obstacle and opportunity and are able to turn both to their advantage.'

Niccolò Machiavelli

———

'The link between my experience as an entrepreneur and that of a politician is all in one word: freedom.'

Silvio Berlusconi

———

'Nobody talks of entrepreneurship as survival, but that's exactly what it is and what nurtures creative thinking.'

Anita Roddick

———

'It is not sufficient that I succeed – all others must fail.'

Genghis Khan

———

The notion that an entrepreneur has an inbuilt ability to turn adversity into good fortune is something I find really annoying. I have a friend who is a banker. He's managed to work his way up from a tough Liverpool estate to being managing director of a Canadian merchant bank on a salary that boggles the mind. Now *that's* overcoming adversity and turning it into good fortune, but he's not technically an entrepreneur. He likes having a job and a boss and he loves his end-of-year bonus, the last of which enabled him to retire at the ripe old age of 35. Similarly I know someone who is married to a wealthy city chap who has set herself up as an art consultant flogging high end contemporary works to his mates. No adversity to overcome whatsoever and a very tidy living by simply leveraging some contacts. In principle she is an entrepreneur but where is the risk and toil that everyone associates with it? The whole notion of what constitutes an entrepreneur is slightly mixed up, and Branson and his hot air balloons and space adventures isn't exactly helping. Branson is a superstar and doesn't really represent the entrepreneurs that I know.

Here's what the *Oxford English Dictionary* has to say on the subject:

En·tre·pre·neur

– noun

person who undertakes commercial venture.

Now being a failure and not famous what I have to say on the matter has absolutely no credence. Pithy quotes only really work if you've made it – who wants advice from someone who failed? Surely that would be bad advice. However, you've forked out £9.99 for this book so I'm assuming you must have a scintilla of interest in my point of view. And since I'm sitting on this, the writer's side of the desk, I'm going to give it to you anyway. If you don't want to know, look away now.

Firstly, I don't think that an entrepreneur is better than anyone else. I think the term should be treated as some sort of affliction rather than a term of admiration. It's proven that many entrepreneurs exhibit mild psychopathic tendencies and often the motive for working for yourself is that it offers you a life comparatively free of external discipline. Aside from chopping up their college chums and putting them in the deep-freeze for laughing at them, the other thing psychopaths don't like is external discipline, you see.

Most entrepreneurs simply don't fit into the rigid structure that modern life requires of us. And this is what makes us what we are. Many people engaged in entrepreneurial pursuits do so because they can't get a job anywhere else. We're the misfits of the world and some of us end up running it whilst others end up flogging lighters from a suitcase outside the betting shop on a Saturday afternoon.

Between these extremes many of us toil away running small internet retail stores, sandwich shops and carpet cleaning franchises, content in the knowledge that there is nobody breathing down our necks at 9 a.m. on a grey Monday morning. Freedom is the motive, and I'm with Silvio Berlusconi on this one. We don't necessarily do it for the prospect of a super yacht on the Med with a troupe of glamorous models. We do it to be free.

Furthermore, entrepreneurialism does not necessarily bring you happiness or wealth; indeed nearly all the entrepreneurs I know earn less than their salaried counterparts and get less sleep. If the buck stops with you there is no respite, you bring it home and you think about it in the back of your mind even while you're having Sunday lunch with your friends in a cool pub in Twickenham. Some people use the word entrepreneur as if it's a great achievement in itself. I've even met people who put it on their business cards as if it's a mark of honour. It's not. Anybody with internet access, the ability to read and a credit card can start a limited company by the end of the day, and hey presto you're MD of your own business. Entrepreneurialism is a state of mind rather than some modern day embodiment of Drake or Magellan.

So here's my definition of what I think a true entrepreneur is: an entrepreneur weighs up frightening and risky against poor and free and sees the latter. Some of us measure richness in terms of money, others measure it in terms of freedom and a small percentage of us get both. But here's the thing I learnt. There is actually nothing to be afraid of. Five months into the venture, struggling for cash, a new wife, big mortgage, half renovated terrace, kiddie on the way, all this on my plate and I wasn't frightened. In fact I found the experience utterly exhilarating. I had nothing to fall back on but myself and nothing focuses the mind like that. I'm with Anita Roddick on that one. The pressure makes you creative, it spurs you on.

Once you make the first leap into the unknown and are responsible for your own pay packet it's amazing how quickly you forget how terrifying the idea of it was. In many ways you're disappointed you didn't do it years ago. Once you're off the treadmill you don't ever have to get back on.

Anyway, I was living on the edge, poorer than ever but rich in my work. I didn't need permission from anyone to do anything and it felt good. The blood was pumping through my veins, I felt alive and in control and we were going to get the money to keep the business going. Rowan and I decided to contact everyone we knew one last time, all guns blazing, to find our knights in shining armour. We gave it one big final push.

We emailed and called everyone we knew telling them of the situation, and a few days later Rowan's uncle called up to say that he had met someone at his London club who might be interested in investing. He didn't know too much about them but he provided us with a phone number and Rowan made the call.

We sat there nervously and Rowan got through to our man, Mr Big (not his real name, obviously, we agreed that his investment would be a secret). She was brilliant. Passionate, bright, engaging. All the things I had first thought when I met her.

As she spoke to him her face was lit up as she sensed the positive vibes from the end of the phone. She told him all about what had happened and what we were trying to do.

'So?' I said, when she'd finished talking.

'Looks very exciting; we've got to post them a business plan to this address,' she said writing it down on the back of an envelope.

Bugger posting, these were desperate times. I looked on the scrap of paper and could see that their offices were just behind Marble Arch. A 15 minute stroll from our flea pit office.

Excited and with much haste, I walked down to Borders on Oxford Street and picked up a very professional looking faux leather binder. I wanted to give the impression that we were dependable sort of people, the sort of people who would write you a letter thanking you for dinner, the sort of people who would pay you back the £10 they borrowed from you on Friday straight away rather than having to be reminded. I wanted a binder that said 'you can trust us, we're honest and reliable and we won't spend your money on mojitos and ladies with loose morals.' But I also wanted a binder that said 'we're young and aggressive and if it were legal would not have to think twice about razing a mid-sized market town to the ground and executing all its inhabitants'. The faux leather folder did that, I thought.

Meanwhile we printed off the latest copy of the business plan on some premium posh paper I had nicked from the EPS printer. The plan was looking splendid. Michael had redone all the cash flow and profit and loss forecasts forward for the next four years, based on the assumption that we would get the investment in July.

A business plan has to have quite a lot of information. We had come a long way since our early attempt and Michael had taught me wisely. I felt like Luke in the opening scenes of *Return of the Jedi*, confident with his light sabre and carrying off the black cape in a way that would never have been possible in *The Empire Strikes Back*. Michael, my own Yoda, sat wisely in the background, should I falter.

I'm aware I might be straying into quite boring territory here. If you've ever written a business plan or never have an intention of doing so then skip over to the next page. If you would like to know what you need to include in a business plan then read on.

Essential things an entrepreneur needs to cover in a business plan are:

1   Executive summary – the introduction to the company written by the MD which gives a summary to each of the main sections that you are about to cover.

2   Nature of the business – this gives a detailed account of what it is you actually do.

3   The management team – who the key people running the business are, where they come from and what they do.

4   The market – this is a breakdown of your customers, revenue streams and future revenue opportunities.

5   Personnel – details on the rest of the team and any subcontractors you may use.

6   Financial analysis – information on your financial performance to date and a revenue and cash flow forecast going forward for four years. You might want to do a couple of scenarios to illustrate how things would pan out if things don't go to plan. We didn't do this bit. It's a shame because if we had we might have asked for more money.

7   SWOT analysis – this is where you stand back from your business and assess the Strengths, Weaknesses, Opportunities and Threats that come to bear on the enterprise.

Be concise and don't waffle. It needs enough information to prick their interest and give the potential investor a good flavour of you and your business, but it shouldn't need a fork lift truck to deliver otherwise you'll lose them. Thirty pages is a good target to aim for.

So your business plan will tell a prospective investor how and what you're going to do with his dosh, plus it proves you can write and add things up which is always useful when you're asking him for a quarter of a million quid. Our business plan was, as they would say in the lads mags, the mutt's nuts. I do not think there would have been a better plan anywhere in London that day and I was confident that I had done the best job I could.

I clutched it, clad in its faux leather folder, to my chest as I stood on the steps of a very impressive vast Edwardian townhouse behind Marble Arch. I rang the bell, nervous, hands slightly sweaty. I was let in by a disembodied and very efficient sounding voice on the squawk box on the wall. I nervously stepped into a cavernous reception room where a sophisticated girl sat alone at a very organized and expensive-looking desk. She spoke in a clipped, confident manner that made me think she was used to dealing with very rich people. I explained I was dropping off something for Mr Big. I then thought she might think I was a courier and panicked.

'I'm, er, not a courier.'

She smiled pityingly.

'Yeah, I'm a business associate, dropping off a proposal for Mark.'

Same expression.

I handed over the faux leather folder. She didn't look at it. She seemed unimpressed but remained attentive.

'Yeah, I own a magazine.' [Stop talking, you idiot.]

She continued to smile.

I managed to stop myself talking more rubbish. She didn't actually care who I was but it made me feel good knowing that this beautiful woman did not think I was a guy who rides around on a motorbike all day looking furious.

I burst back out into the May sunshine and walked back to the office, feeling happy that our potential investors had such great reception rooms and attractive and astute receptionists. Perhaps in a few years' time it might rub off on me and I could have these things. Receptions are important. They say a lot about a business and I've been in a few over the years. We had a manky sofa as a reception area which said a lot about our business. It said we were poor and couldn't afford nice furniture. At IPC, the UK's biggest magazine company, the reception is cold and harsh and there are security men on the door who look as if they could kill you with a pencil. You're not sure if it's the staff or visitors who they are against but they're not happy. Richard

Desmond's *Express* reception is vast, like an aircraft hanger, and there seem to be lots of people in it doing things but nobody seems happy – I wouldn't want to work there. Felix Dennis, the publishing tycoon, has goldfish in his office in a big tank and the receptionists seem genuinely happy and a little cheeky which makes you think it's probably a nice company to work for. When I'm rich I'm going to have a reception like Mr Big: small, modern, friendly, with a very attractive receptionist.

We waited for a week and there was no news. I didn't want to appear too pushy and at the same time I was afraid that they would not be interested. In many ways, not knowing left a glimmer of hope, and I knew that this was our only real live funding opportunity. If they said no, then the opportunity would be extinguished and that would spell doom. It felt cowardly but I could not accept bad news, so we waited. I couldn't think about anything else and didn't really do that much. Poshtotty needed some attention as we had all the models lined up, the website was designed and my partners were itching to get cracking on it. I couldn't concentrate on it because without the funding the business was finished. Obviously I couldn't tell the rest of the Poshtotty team the truth about our perilous fiscal position, and they were grumbling and getting impatient.

Finally I could take no more and I called him on his direct line. Mr Big picked up the phone, and spoke in the tone that only truly confident self-made people have. He was friendly and easy to talk to. And he liked it! He actually liked it.

After all the timewasters and charlatans and rejections and blokes called Norm@n I actually had someone on the end of the phone who was both rich and interested. It didn't get much better than that. Mr Big wanted to come to the office to meet us.

Mr Big was one of a group of three guys who had made millions out of property. I was later informed by a not very reliable source that they were worth about half a billion pounds. Each. In high rolling terms these boys were stratospheric. They were ferociously private, which unfortunately precludes me from naming them. Whether they were worth £1.5 billion or not they are without doubt the coolest people I have ever met in business and, despite their wealth, I've never seen them mentioned once in the business press. And I read a lot of business press. They were everything I wanted to be in business and I now know I won't. So many rich people have crushing, overbearing egos and need to be better than anyone else. Mr Big was the epitome of a self-deprecating, self-made man. Confident, intelligent and he listened. Rowan was clearly smitten. I think I was too.

His chauffeur was parked outside on the double yellow and he entered our shabby little office. I had asked the team to tidy up but there was really very little we could do to make it look good. In fact our poor Dickensian working conditions probably worked in our favour as one thing that most investors hate is ostentatious waste and you could certainly not accuse us of that. He listened as we went through the history of the magazine and our plans for development.

There were lots of questions and it was clear that he had very quickly understood the dynamics of the business.

'Right', he said. 'I like it.'

Rowan and I were finding it hard to control our excitement but tried to remain cool.

'A couple of things,' he continued. 'Firstly, are you sure £200k is enough?'

Two hundred thousand pounds seemed to us like such a massive sum of money that we could not envisage needing any more. We assured him that it was absolutely enough. I have since learnt that when you are dealing with billionaire types the difference between £200k and £300k is not a lot. I mean it's a lot in your wallet, or a lot if you convert it into pub lunches, but in the scheme of investing in stuff it doesn't really make a huge difference. If you've put aside a few million quid to essentially gamble on business ventures then the difference of £100k isn't going to faze you. I didn't know that and most entrepreneurs don't either, so it's a common mistake not to ask for enough money. Many investors actually invest simultaneously in a range of businesses. It spreads the risk because for every ten enterprises you invest in, four will go bust, four will trundle along, one will do quite well and one will explode like a supernova and pay for all the other nine and hopefully a lot more. Had I known that I would have asked for £300k but naively we nodded enthusiastically like children not wanting to put the deal at risk by asking for more cash.

'Secondly, I want your finance guy to run through the numbers with me and my partners,' he finished. We agreed a date two weeks hence where I could wheel Michael in.

'Thirdly, I want my accountants to perform a due diligence.'

'Of course,' we replied. Inside I was thinking, 'what on god's earth is due diligence? Sounds like some sort of medical procedure.'

Now Mr Griffiths, can you please bend over while I perform due diligence on you with this large metal probe.

'And last thing, when do you need the money?'

'End of June,' Rowan and I replied in unison.

Things were looking up. The meeting ended the inertia that I had been feeling over the past week and my confidence soared in the knowledge that I could now plan for the future of the company. It turned out that due diligence was not a rectal probing procedure but an exercise whereby the buyer or investor of a business does a thorough check on the facts that the business owner has provided. Sometimes they will also check you and key members of staff out personally to ensure there are no skeletons lurking in cupboards.

Michael rang me. He was not happy. Just because we had found someone interested it didn't mean we should stop our fundraising activities because pretty soon they were likely to be *not* interested and then we would have spent our time courting this one frog – and when it hopped off there wouldn't be any others left on the lily pond. The frog analogy was starting to grate. I was sure that these guys were the ticket. Michael was having none of it; we needed to have as many balls in the air as possible, and alongside the option of floating the company to the readers he had come up with another plan. The SFLG.

The Small Firms Loan Guarantee Scheme was set up by the DTI to enable business to borrow money. Generally speaking the banks will not lend you anything unless you give them your house as a guarantee. Fine if you have a house of course. Now what happens if all you have is a rented caravan. Or a tent.

Bank Manager: 'Hello Miss Smith, come in, sit down, tea? How can I help you?'

Miss Smith: 'I would like to borrow £75,000 to import golf trolleys from China.'

Bank manager: 'Splendid. Now a few questions. Do you have a house with £75,000 equity so that if it goes wrong we can get our money back?'

Miss Smith: 'Er, no. I live in a teepee.'

Bank Manager: 'Please leave the building. Now. SECU-RITY!'

As I have said before, banks don't like risk. We knew that if we went to the bank and asked to borrow £250k then we would be asked to give them the deeds of our houses as guarantee, and neither Rowan nor I wanted to put our homes on the line.

So a few years ago the Department of Trade and Industry dreamt up the SFLG Scheme for people who don't have lots of money lying around to pump into businesses or houses they could give the bank as guarantee. The way the scheme works is that you approach your friendly bank drone with your business plan. If they like it, rather than ask if you have a house to the value of the loan you are asking for, the government will provide a guarantee for 75 per cent of the loan. Therefore if you want £100k from the bank, they're only risking £25k. Banks like this sort of thing because it fits nicely with their no risk philosophy. The government (or you the taxpayer) takes the big risk. The bank is still risking something so they don't give them out willy-nilly but, since reducing risk is what they are all about, your average bank manager is more likely to give you a loan under this scheme. The SFLG Scheme is capped at £250k. Optimistically we asked for £250k.

We filled out forms. Many forms. We provided our profit and loss forecasts for the next four years. We sat through an interrogation from our bank manager for two hours. They said they would let us know in due course. I assumed they had to feed it into the central brain for a decision. From the look on their faces and my past experience with my media friendly bank manager I expected the usual negative reply.

I had been treading water while I worried about funding matters and now things were pressing. We had to get back to the business of launching Poshtotty. Rowan was working hard on the summer edition of the *Erotic Review*, a combined issue for June and July, so that we could all have a break and supposedly go on hols. Obviously at this stage a holiday was well out of the question. Sally had worked out a marketing campaign that could go live as soon as the money came in. The business leapt back into life as the threat of imminent demise looked like it had been lifted. The meeting to run through the financials was in the diary for the following Friday and Michael and I knew the numbers inside out and back to front. We needed to know what our margins were, breakeven point, advertising revenue and circulation payroll, and everything was committed to memory. Now I could get on and run the business.

So Poshtotty was ready to roll and we needed a venue. Anticipating our expected investment I went for broke, dipped into the last of our cash and set about putting together my first ever photo shoot.

I am always amazed how well organized things are when you delve into a new business. Like with hiring the models, I had never given any thought whatsoever to where these things are shot. I thought since it was important that the whole thing was posh it would be right and proper to hire a country house of some description. There are websites which actually specialize in representing people who live in houses that can be used for photo shoots. I was trying to find something manor-ish in the south east and it became clear very quickly that at £10,000 for a day this was not really going to be workable. We fleetingly had someone who was a friend of a friend, said we could borrow theirs, but then bottled out when they discovered we were going to be turning up with a minibus full of glamour models who would be getting naked throughout the day while Triggers and I photographed them. In the end I found a house in the East End of London which was done up beautifully, and from the photos it looked like Lawrence Llewelyn-Bowen had been detonated in there. Even better I could rent it by the hour. I figured we could get ten models shot, and nail the whole thing before lunch time.

We were able to arrange the shoot for the coming Friday and Pauline booked the girls in. It was a miserable, drizzly morning. I set off for the house with some trepidation at having to venture into this very grim part of town.

It was a large Edwardian terrace next to a Halfords bike shop on the Mile End Road. Mile End is the second worse place in the world. There's a Bolivian salt mine that's worse apparently. The phrase urban decay was invented for this part of London and the area is defined by third-rate housing, gang crime, ethnic tension and the icing on the cake is a dual carriageway running straight through the middle. Thirty-two ton articulated lorries roar along it on their way to Tilbury, and the air is thick with choking fumes and noise. In amongst all this are thrown the uneducated and poor which gives the place a threatening, intimidating feel. Mile End is not posh. Our location house was overlooking this stretch of road and didn't look particularly posh from the outside either.

However, it did have its benefits. It was cheap. At £100 an hour it came in a lot less than the stately home. It was close to London which means the models could come by tube. I had been informed that it is customary to refund the models for their travel expenses and since they were all London-based it was only a couple of quid each to get them to the venue. We had agreed to pay £50 an hour on the basis that we would need each one for a maximum of two hours. Afterwards I found out that we were paying a bit over the odds and learnt that you can get a low profile porn actress to do a whole film for £150 a go.

We had also asked the models to bring their own kit which was going to save me a few bob. Triggers was waiting outside looking nervous. His fiancée was with him – she had offered to help with styling – and we also hired a make-up artist to try to posh things up a bit. I knocked at the door and a small, rather effete looking skinny fellow with round specs answered the door holding a very silly shitsu dog. He was taking the kids off to school and informed us that we had until 1 p.m. to get it all shot. Him and his wife were going out for the morning but they were going to leave the dog if that was OK. It was, and Triggers looked at me and winked; we both knew that the dog would end up being a prop in our photo shoot that day.

We were invited down into the kitchen. This was going to be the base, where the girls would get made up and Triggers' missus would style each of the models to look like minor royalty. Pauline had turned up with a box full of coats and dresses which Rowan and the team had lent us.

I popped out to the shop and bought half a dozen bottles of Champagne. I thought if we could get everyone relaxed it would make the day go better. Apart from anything else I think Triggers and I were so nervous we needed a stiffener to get us going.

The doorbell rang at 9 o'clock. Pauline went up and answered it. Nicole came down the stairs, obligatory wheeled suitcase thumping and bumping behind her. We all looked around nervously, all novices, all slightly unsure of ourselves. Nicole broke the ice. 'Shall we get going, I 'ave anozer interview at two', she explained in a thick French accent. Then the doorbell rang again and Lavinia and Blade came down together. Elizabeth, petite, 70, Blade 6ft7, West Indian, 25.

The kitchen suddenly seemed very crowded as Trigger's fiancée starting pulling costumes together and the make-up girl opened her big vanity case. I downed a glass of champagne and the girls started to strip and get changed into their finery in the middle of the chaos. Triggers and I fled out to the garden to have a fag. I don't smoke, but inhaling smoke in the yard of the house was preferable to being in the kitchen while models got naked all around me. I mean, I was about to be a father.

Despite the squalor outside, the inside of the house was incredible. Everything was perfectly thought out and the fabric and paint and objects all came together in the most stylish way. How these people brought up two kids here is beyond me.

Triggers and I talked about what we were going to do with each shoot.

Each girl needed about 30 photographs. We would photo-graph them sweeping into the room looking posh, nose in the air with the sort of conceited arrogance that old money seems to possess. Their seventeenth-century ancestor had shagged a king's cousin and accordingly been given half of Shropshire for the trouble, so of course that entitled them to think they were better than you four centuries later. They've earned it. The girls would strip with nose held high, disdainfully looking down at Triggers and we would shoot the whole thing. On the site, when it went live, you would be able to see the first couple of the pictures. The rest would be behind a payment gate. If you were a paid subscriber you got to see the other 28 shots which obviously concluded with the lady in all her naked glory. Twenty-five quid a week well spent.

Fairly simple I thought. Except not that simple. The problem lay with our lack of porn shoot etiquette. Triggers, like myself, is a well brought up young man and when a lady who is not your girlfriend or wife undresses in a room, your initial reaction is to look away. If we had taken it to its logical conclusion then we would have preferred the girls to photograph themselves and we would simply not have had to face the embarrassing prospect of actually telling them what to do. Fortunately, Lavinia from Sloane Square stepped up and took control. Exceedingly posh, with that slow sort of drawl that makes you think she is dying of ennui, she explained how the shoot was going to go. Being 70, we obviously didn't want a full naked shot from her (the humanity), but she was extremely game and to this day my favourite Poshtotty shot is one of Lavinia in basque, stockings and suspenders standing regally in front of a four-poster bed.

Nicole was not so easy and I explained to her in the hall that I wanted her to walk in as if she owned half of France. Nicole didn't own much beyond her wheeled suitcase so consequently walked in with her nose in the air and face sort of scrunched up. She awkwardly tripped around the room and when she got down to her bra and pants clearly didn't want to go any further. I left the room thinking I might have been the problem but five minutes later Triggers came out looking fairly glum shaking his head.

'Slight problem, er, this is her first time and she's not mad about going any further.'

'Shit' I said. 'OK, not to worry, she's pretty so we can use these shots for publicity.' So I called down the stairs to the kitchen to send up the next one.

Blade was truly beautiful, tall, a professional model, and knew exactly what she was doing. Pauline, Triggers' fiancée and the make-up girl had done a great job with a large feather in her hair and a boa. I felt I was hitting my stride now and was in the room when she walked in. I would direct the shoot up until the point it got a bit naked where I would leave the room and Triggers would do the rest. Blade informed us that she was at that time suffering from a rash and was fairly reluctant to go beyond knickers.

So for the first three models we had a grand total of zero nude shots and I was about £300 down. I realized that I had to take control of the situation. I called in Pauline.

Pauline rushed up the stairs, her usual overwhelming happiness driven to a new plateau of joy by the cold, early morning injection of cheap corner-shop champagne. It was lost on me because I was cross and worried about the poor investment I had made up to this point.

'Yes, how can I help you?' asked Pauline, talking to me as if we had just met.

'Out of three photo sets we've got precisely zero naked shots for our naked posh lady website that launches on Friday.'

'Hmm, I can see your problem.'

'No, Pauline, it's OUR problem. I need someone who can talk to these girls in no uncertain terms and inform them that removal of undergarments is mandatory. Repeat mandatory. I mean, we did tell them all it was a nude photo shoot?'

'Uhu, yup I told 'em,' she replied.

'Well you've got to go down and tell them how it is. I don't care if they're shy, 'on', have a rash, are a man; we need nudity otherwise this whole thing is a waste of time. I want them coming up those stairs knowing they are getting naked. Don't send anyone else up here who isn't prepared to get naked!'

'Righto, boss,' and off she went back downstairs. About 20 seconds later Debbie comes up the stairs, goes into the room and takes off ALL her clothes and we photograph her.

Then we do Kylie, who's dark and mysterious – she strips off and takes a dip in the ornate roll top bath.

Then Katie comes up the stairs and we shoot her in the master bedroom standing in front of a ten-foot high mirror, and just as she's starting her strip, the funny little dog trots past and she picks it up and does the full routine until she is stood in front of the mirror, buck naked holding a rather bewildered looking pooch.

And so it goes on. We shoot two at the same time in the Japanese inspired garden and we've got customers coming out of Halfords who can see through the metal railings as Triggers shoots, shutter whirring again and again, and I find myself on fire shouting 'You fucking own Shropshire, baby!'

By lunchtime we had bagged ten models, were about £1500 in the hole and I thought we had done a fairly good job all in all. We had three underwear photo sets which I would bank for later when the site was established and seven nude photo sets which was enough to get the site up. We were nearly ready for launch.

CHAPTER SIX

The biggest month of my life

Humans are funny about sex. We're hard-wired to do it and think about it all the time, but we don't like to admit it. We think we're civilized; better than animals. We try to control our urges, yet they simmer constantly under the surface in everything we do. Your libido, your drive to procreate is an ancient evolutionary directive as old as time itself that ensures the continuation of our species. You may actually think that your job is important or your house or your hobby, or your hairstyle or what car you drive. Actually none of it is. You might think it's important in your life to write a best-selling novel, produce some groundbreaking art, make a million in the city and sponsor a hospital wing, or leave your mark on humanity in a myriad of ways. But the only mark humanity really needs you to leave is offspring. From a survival of the species perspective you have only one purpose and that's to hook up with someone of the opposite sex and create some genetic material that develops into a child. As a sort of secondary optional directive you're also programmed to stick around with your partner for a bit until that child is old enough to fend for itself. Then, it too can hook up with someone and make more genetic material and the cycle repeats. Five hundred million years of evolution has brought us to this point and the overriding objective of all that evolution is to keep doing it. All the other stuff, like a wide screen telly and a fortnight in the Algarve is nice and makes us feel good, but it's peripheral to the core function of keeping on having sex. Keep making that genetic material. Keep the species going.

So it's no wonder, given this involuntary urge to engage in rumpy pumpy, that the sex industry has been at the forefront in any new communicative medium, particularly since we started relatively sophisticated social interaction about two and a half a million years ago. Man's first big communication step was speech. Now we can't really be sure of what our Neanderthal forebears talked about around the fire because they forgot to write it down, but I'll bet you a hundred quid that the earliest conversations were about sex:

'Ug, eurgh, oo oo, did you see the hairy set of bazookas on that little minx?'

'Urg urg, ooh, ooh, nah mate, I'm more of a protruding forehead kinda guy.'

So we move on a few hundred millennia and early humans start to learn to draw rudimentary figures on cave walls. What's one of the first things they draw about? People having a bit of slap and tickle. And hunting, which is effectively eating. So they write about food and sex. Chuck in a section on travel and some pictures of Sting's new summer house in the Hamptons and you've got the *Sunday Times*. On a wall.

Fast forward again to 2000 BC where, on the shores of the Nile, the Egyptians were busy outlining their sexual preferences in graphic detail on the inner walls of the temples and leaving them lying around sketched on bits of papyri.

Around 1450, Johannes Gutenberg invented movable type printing which made books easier to make and distribute, and within a year filthy writing hit the market, albeit on the quiet because if you were caught with it you could have your nose cut off. Then, around 1880, George Eastman invented the modern camera and suddenly people could take their own pictures with a device that would fit in your pocket. *Readers Wives* started about a week later. In 1895 Louis Lumiere invented the portable film camera and by the end of the nineteenth century there was already a healthy market for 'stag' films (as the early porn film became known), so called because they were usually shown to groups of men. Interestingly, by 1910, Germany was the world's leading producer of fetish films. And getting ready to decimate Europe.

Then the home video came along and porn really started to fly as you could watch real people at it in the comfort of your own home. And this is interesting: I've heard it said that one of the reasons that VHS won the war against Betamax format was because the latter refused to license any porn films.

Finally, in the late 1990s, the internet reached the masses. Today it's possible to find whatever peculiar fantasy turns you on and deliver it in seconds to your desk. You don't even have to walk down to the porn shop and worry about coming out the door and seeing Mrs Perkins from number 44 on her way back from bingo. And you don't have to have embarrassing conversations with the spotty, long-haired youth who works there and is practically comatose through excessive masturbation.

You can have the most kinky desires and you'll find them online. At the time of writing, one of the biggest new sites on the internet is Youporn.com, a site where not only can you find every single sex act known to man, but you can upload pictures of yourself having sex. And it's all free. Well they did say that the internet would deliver true democratization of information, and its origins are traceable in a line right back to a drawing on a cave wall.

So, following in the long tradition of jumping onto a new medium with a sexually explicit proposition, I found myself in the peculiar position of being an internet sex pioneer. I was bringing a new genre of titillation to a new medium. I didn't tell my mother about this, obviously.

The raw materials for Poshtotty were in place. The web guy had put together a site that could take money from people's credit card which would enable them to see the naked bits. It was a standard template so that as the site grew he only had to drop more images in as he went.

We also started to write the biographies for the girls which were, of course, completely fabricated even down to the names.

Camilla Ogden Smyth, 42, Sloane Square

Camilla is a member of the Kensington Rotary Club, and on the board of the Royal Ballet. She likes to spend her free time shopping in Paris or Rome. Camilla is inordinately posh. When not undertaking charitable duties, Camilla likes to take off all her clothes.

Each one had a similar description underneath the main picture. If you wanted to see Camilla take her clothes off then you had to register and pay your £25 monthly fee.

Triggers had downloaded the camera files to his computer and, using the magic of Photoshop, had erased tattoos and belly piercings, which nearly everyone had. Some teeth had been whitened and a couple of zits had been deleted. By Thursday, the site was ready to go live and we waited nervously as our tech man uploaded the files. I sat anxiously refreshing my computer screen, which was showing a blank page. After about two minutes the screen came alive with colour, the vivid Poshtotty logo at the top and there to the left were four of our posh ladies, fully clothed and looking not too shabby. We were in business. Now all we had to do was wait for the cash to roll in.

Sign ups were very slow to begin with, and I knew from my experience with the first dotcom business that I was involved in that launching a site is only the first step to being an internet millionaire. The most important thing you need to do is tell people about it.

Many people mistakenly think that setting up a web business requires little more than a concept and the services of a web design company. Take for example the amount of people who in recent years have set up websites selling adult sex toys.

On paper, to the would-be entrepreneur, it looks brilliant:

- Cost of website to build   £5000

- Cost of rabbit vibrator wholesale   £5

- Retail price of a rabbit vibrator   £25

On the assumption that I charge out post and packaging at cost and turn the front room into a storage and fulfillment area, I've worked out that if I sell 3000 rabbits I'll make £60,000. Sixty grand! That's bloody twice what I make working at the council office and I wouldn't have to take orders from that twat Mr Cheadle. Christ, why didn't I do this earlier. That's it, come Monday I'm packing in my job and I'm going to sell rabbit vibrators for a living.

Except you shouldn't. I mean, you'll know by now that I'm very pro breaking away and doing it on your own, but risks should be considered and in any consumer business you need to work out how much it costs to bring your product to market. By all means take risks, but this business idea does not factor in that it's a brutally competitive market and that your rivals are probably spending £20k a week on online and offline marketing. Without investment in marketing you will launch your website and about three months down the road you will close it, not having sold a single item.

It's the same with a plethora of businesses. I know a guy in his late twenties who drives around in a top-of-the-range Aston Martin. He runs a dating website. And before you think, excellent, I'll start a dating website and pop down to the new Aston showroom on Saturday, you should consider that this guy started the business from scratch using his credit card two years ago and has continuously reinvested his return to the point that he currently spends about £100,000 a month advertising on Google.

An internet shop is like any other shop. It'll cost you to deck it out, you'll need some stock and then you need to tell people about it, otherwise you'll never get off the mark.

To succeed, Poshtotty was going to need some promotion and this was where my PR partner, Roberta, was going to come in.

I'm standing outside the incredibly impressive office of our hopefully soon-to-be investor with Michael. He's sweating and slightly breathless because he walked here from Hammersmith which is about five miles away, and it's mid June.

It's crunch time. The PLC option would take months to turn around, plus we would need cash to print up and send out prospectuses and pay the necessary accountants and do all the official stuff. Furthermore, 'The Bank That Likes To Say No' had, er, said 'no' that very morning to the SFLG scheme, which hadn't come as a surprise. Just once it would have been nice for them to say yes to something. This really was the only show in town, and everything came down to this meeting and what happened over the next few hours.

The bank account was at zero. It was two weeks to pay day, I had got to pay the printer six grand for doing the last magazine job. The writers and illustrators were chasing me for payment and I had irresponsibly blown our last grand and a half on hiring a house and photographing a bunch of glamour models stripping off. I was a fortnight away from being a father. Talk about living life on the edge. I shook my head to block out the growing feeling of panic. I took a deep breath and rang the buzzer.

The posh receptionist buzzed us in and the reception was cool with air conditioning. I was wearing a suit this time so there was not going to be any confusion about me being a biker. For that I was relieved and I informed her that we were there to see Mr Big. She asked us if we wanted a drink. I asked for tea, Michael plumped for water. He looked so hot I thought he was going to burst into flames. She showed us into the boardroom.

Wow. You could have fit our office into this boardroom three times. The table could have sat 40. All I felt was awe. There was a huge map on the wall of something. It represented domination. A map of things these guys had dominated, perhaps? The world? It was difficult to know where to sit at such a big table so we decided to stay at the end nearest the door. I took my jacket off and got my papers out.

The door knocked, I sat upright and a chef in a tall white hat, tunic and blue checked trousers walked in with tea and water. They had a chef in the building to make tea. What kind of people had a full time chef in the office making tea? I mean, I could barely afford to have anyone on the payroll let alone someone as seemingly superfluous as a chef. To make tea. I sipped mine from a fine china cup. The door opened and Mr Big walked in followed by his partner.

I was nervous but at the same time I was confident that I knew my stuff. This was clearly the business end of the deal and I missed not having Rowan with me. She was my partner and together we gave off great energy; it felt wrong her not being here. There was so much riding on this, the future of the business, my job, the team, the writers, the respect of my dad, Sally and Rowan. I simply could not let them down.

Nice, charming Mr Big had changed into hardnosed, deal-maker Mr Big and it was clear that you don't amass half a billion without being sharp where it counts. The numbers were picked apart, sliced and diced in every way and they tested our knowledge of the business to the max. Michael sweetened the deal by making any potential investment eligible for EIS relief. EIS is the Enterprise Initiative Scheme which was set up by the government to encourage people to invest in small firms that may struggle to find investment elsewhere (what with the banks and their propensity to say no to start-up companies that might be seen as risky). Any company can apply to be registered as an EIS company providing they fulfill the appropriate criteria, and your accountant should be able to tell you if your firm is eligible. If a company is EIS approved, an individual investor can put in up to £100k and get 20 per cent tax relief on the investment. This means the investment is only costing him £80k. Also, there is tax relief on any capital gain made with that investment. So if the business is sold the money he makes on the exit is tax free.

Half an hour later we had been through every item of income and even more thoroughly every item of cost. I felt like I'd been put through a mincer, but we hadn't slipped up once and I was confident we'd done a good job. There was a lull in conversation and Mr Big asked:

'So is there anyone else interested?'

'I'll be honest,' I lied, trying to stay cool and not think about our zero bank balance, 'there is one other party interested in investing.'

'And we're at quite an advanced stage,' lied Michael further.

'Well I think we'd better get cracking then,' continued Mr Big and with that he rose from his chair and concluded the meeting.

Seconds later I was once again standing outside in the sunshine feeling confused and a bit frazzled.

'Beer. I need a pint of strong, cold beer,' I said to Michael. We walked in silence until we found a pub in a little mews street around the corner. I sat down on a small iron chair outside the front and Michael went in to get the drinks. The life of London in full summer buzzed around me and I buzzed along with it. I took a big swig of my pint. 'Did we just do a fucking deal?'

'I think we did,' Michael said.

'Cheers,' we both said in harmony and I kicked back my chair and looked into the sun, letting it warm my face.

And that was it. It was a yes. I was ecstatic and rang Rowan to tell her the good news.

'I'm not wanting to put a dampener on this,' said Michael, putting a dampener on it as we walked back to the office, 'but we have to draw up contracts first and that's going to take some time. Then they're sending their due diligence guy in. The deal's not a deal until the money is in the bank. I think we should keep looking for more investors.'

Bollocks to the contract. We had a deal, we were going to get out two hundred grand and I was going to be a million-aire. I could start going to dinner parties again.

First guest: 'So what do you do Gavin?'

Gavin: [Entire dinner party stops mid-conversation to listen to my reply] 'I am the richest magazine publisher in Europe.'

First guest: 'Oh, I'm just a merchant banker.'

Second guest: 'What do you drive?'

Gavin: 'I don't. I fly.'

They think it's all over, it is now, Griffiths brings it home, what a comeback.

I rushed back to the office to share the good news with the team. We put the answerphone on and spent the rest of the afternoon in the Academy playing wink murder, drinking red wine and discussing what title we should launch next.

Or perhaps we should start acquiring businesses as it was less risky in the long term. It was the highpoint of my career thus far. We sat at our regular table and we drank until the small hours planning great campaigns and pledging that we would be together forever.

I woke the next morning with my body quivering. Too many cigars and too much red wine and being over 30. I couldn't do it like this anymore and function the next day. It had seemed like only yesterday when I first came to London and you could go out every night, drink all night, eat badly and there you were bright as a button at 9 a.m. the next morning ready to do it all again. I tore myself out of bed, Katharine next to me looking big and beautiful. The baby really could be born any minute so it was crucial that I get everything tied up before that happened. We also had ten days until the payroll was due. Generally speaking if you miss a payroll in business you're pretty well stuffed. It's the unwritten rule, and any decent business owner will know that this is the one payment you don't ever mess with. If you miss the salary date your staff will be gone. I knew that we had to have the money by then.

I struggled into work, head sore, nausea rising; feeling claustrophobic on the tube I jumped off a few stops early to get some air and avoid puking up on the guy standing next to me. I swung by Coffee Republic and scored a double espresso to try to wake myself up. While there I saw a new book on the counter top near the till called *Anyone Can Do It* written by the founders of Coffee Republic. 'They can,

can't they,' I mused to myself and I made a mental note to ring them as fellow entrepreneurs and tell them about my latest magazine idea, which was going to be a title called *Entrepreneur*. For entrepreneurs, naturally.

The coffee made me jangly and sped up and intensified my hangover which knackered any sort of concentration. This was a shame because Michael was sitting at my desk waiting for me with the sole intention of making me concentrate. He had sneaked off earlier the night before, being wiser and more sensible than I, and had a boiler plate (or standard) shareholder agreement up on my PC ready to modify. He was tapping his foot impatiently and looked annoyed as I plumped down on the chair opposite him. None of the other *Erotic Review* staff had made it in yet and it was about 9.30.

There are certain things you need to agree in a shareholder agreement.

1   How much money they are putting in.

2   How many shares they are getting in return.

3   Key staff obligations (and they need to have contracts of employment).

We sketched out the contract in draft form and I got one of the work experience people we had in later that day to drop it round to Mr Big's office, or 'The Boys' as they became known.

One problem that had been thrown up was our valuation on the business. If they put in £200k for 30 per cent of the company this valued the business at about £700k. Since we'd purchased it for a quid only a few months before this seemed like quite a lot of money when we hadn't really done that much. Furthermore, Rowan, Sally and myself had put in £55k and this valuation would have seen my investment of £25k suddenly worth £200k. Again, nice to make such a paper profit without doing anything, but not really a fair valuation and The Boys were concerned. To overcome this disparity I suggested that they invest £100k for 30 per cent equity, valuing the business at just over £300k. They then lend the company £100k which we would pay back, plus interest when the cash started rolling in. It didn't really make any difference to me. I just wanted the cash so we could get cracking.

The Boys liked this plan and Michael drew up a loan agreement which would go along with the shareholder agreement.

Now, being super rich, The Boys only used the best accountants and lawyers for their deals. That afternoon I had a call from a senior partner at one of the country's leading accountancy firms to discuss due diligence. Their job is to go through our business with a tooth comb and ascertain if everything we had said up to this point was true. This process does not only mean looking at the books; they will also talk to staff, check your suppliers and generally root around and poke their nose into every aspect of the business to make sure everything stands up. A friend of mine is an accountant, and advised me to tidy the place up because apparently there is much store put in how an office looks, which reflects how a management team functions. Hmmm. He booked an appointment to come that Thursday and I was immediately nervous again. This was a very serious, grown-up company and I was worried that they might flag something that The Boys had not spotted and the whole deal would be off.

Meanwhile there was a magazine that needed to be published, and an erotic website that needed to be launched, and although it was exciting spending all this time talking about investors it was time to get back to work.

Rowan and her team were working on the September issue which was themed Suck-it-on-Sea. Always conscious of cost savings we put a picture of the latest work experience girl and one of Rowan's best chums (the lovely manager of the Academy) Mandana kissing each other on the front cover. We also had one of my favourite comedians writing in the issue – Richard Herring. He used to be part of the double act Lee & Herring on the telly. He was promoting a stand up tour he was doing to rival the very famous *Vagina Monologues*, a surprise hit which took the West End by storm in 2001. His version was 'one for the lads' called *Talking Cock*.

Also there was a brilliant article on Charlie Skelton and Victoria Coren, both great writers who had previously reviewed porn films for our own magazine. Not only was this their last ever review for us, which was sad, but they also let us interview them about their own experiences in making a porn film.

They had written a script, raised some funds, hired some porn actors and shot them and ultimately released a film called *Naughty Twins*. Then they wrote a book called *Once More With Feeling* describing their experience. It was a really fresh and original idea for a book and a really great piece for the magazine.

I also put a full page advert on the back page of the issue promoting Poshtotty. It had a picture of my two favourite tottys and underneath it simply said 'Are you posh enough?'

Thursday came and the due diligence accountant turned up. He was in his early sixties and was a big name in the book publishing world, and presumably had been given our job to deal with because a magazine is sort of a book. He was a judge on various literary panels and knew of Rowan. He sat down with a fairly stern expression on his face and asked Michael some basic rudimentary questions about the accounts, looked through our purchase and sales ledgers, looked at the printing bills to see that we had actually been printing some magazines; the whole thing was feeling rather tense and worrying until Rowan walked in. The frost instantly thawed and his face lit up. This was prime *Erotic*

Review target reader and Rowan completely bewitched him. They chatted about books and people they knew and the whole exchange was one of complete loveliness. I was tempted to invite Pauline in and smother the already saccharine exchange with even more bonhomie, but thought that this might cause overload and lead to our man simply exploding with pleasure. Which might delay our funding. To our absolute relief Michael and I were completely sidelined from the conversation and no more was said about accounts or the business. In fact that was pretty much the end of our involvement in the process. After half an hour of Rowan treatment the man was like a content little puppy; I thought he was going to lie down and have his tummy tickled. He had been thoroughly worked over and when his defences were completely removed Rowan delivered the killer question: 'So, what are you going to report back?'

'Oh, everything here is fine. You have a lovely little business. If you don't mind I'm going to suggest to your new investors that I become your auditing accountants,' he replied. Any excuse to come and have lunch occasionally with Rowan, I thought cynically.

We got Pauline to walk him to the elevator. A sated man left the Erotic Towers that day and reported back to The Boys that we were a sound bet.

Roberta had been very busy ringing all her press contacts to try to get coverage for Poshtotty and there had been some success. The Saturday *Guardian* picked it up and ran a small piece, and various websites ran articles. The following day she rang to say that *FHM*, at the time the largest selling lads monthly, wanted to do a four page feature on the site if we could provide free content. Of course we could bloody provide free content and we emailed over the images and profiles immediately. We would have to wait a good few weeks to see the benefit of this potentially very exciting development but, in the short term, the low-level success started to see traffic to the new site increase almost immediately and in a very short time money was starting to trickle into the account.

Michael was busy with the shareholders' contract batting it back and forth between him and The Boys' lawyers. A young and extremely bright lawyer called Nick Hazel from the very prestigious law firm Taylor Wessing was not letting a single thing slip by, and the shareholder agreement slowly evolved into a document that both sides were happy with.

By Tuesday everything was ready and we were invited over to The Boys' office to sign everything. We walked into the cavernous boardroom and Nick and The Boys were sitting at one end with a massive pile of papers in front of them. Rowan, Michael and I took our seats and innumerable pieces of paper went around the table. Each had to be initialled on every page and signed, and there was a copy of each document for all of the shareholders. Michael at this point put in his invoice for his services up to this point which had been contingent on our finding funding, for which he had been instrumental. We had previously agreed that this invoice would be paid in shares of the company and Michael now become a fellow shareholder. We were busy scribbling for about 20 minutes and suddenly the paper stopped coming around. That was it. The deal was sealed and we had our funding.

Michael gave the lawyers our bank details into which the money would be transferred that very afternoon, and we had a glass of champagne to seal the deal.

Rowan and I left the office and walked into the nearest bar. We then seemed to stop in every bar on the way back to Maddox Street, and the booze, coupled with the relief and joy of doing the deal, flooded over me. To have persuaded someone to give us the money to realize our dreams was an amazing experience. We had gone out there and secured investment for a business from three very successful blokes; they had entrusted us with their money and it was an incredibly uplifting experience.

We spent the afternoon carousing around bars in Soho and by the time we got back to the Academy half the people in there had heard the news and everyone was coming up and patting us on the back and saying well done. Everybody thought that the *Erotic Review* was going to be plain sailing from this point onwards.

Thursday arrived with the anticipated hangover and I checked the bank account online to arrange the transfer of the salaries. The account had £10 in it. What was going on? The money should have been in there yesterday afternoon while we caroused. I rang the lawyers who assured me that the funds had been transferred. I rang our bank who assured me, again, that the funds had not been transferred. I rang Michael. He assured me that he had given them the right account number. Well the cash wasn't in our bloody account!

Five minutes later a very sheepish Michael rang back to say that he had foolishly given them the account number of the *ER* PLC account that we had set up as part of our readers share selling idea. I rang the bank who confirmed that the £200k was indeed sitting in the wrong account. Hmm, great start. We had managed to lose our investment for best part of a morning. I transferred the full amount into our account and paid the salaries. I also paid Pauline for the first time. She was officially part of the family and I was glad that I could finally remunerate her for all her hard work and loyalty up to this point. I had become very attached to Pauline and was glad that she was now part of the team. We paid some angry contributors who were months overdue and then I asked my bank drone if I could set up a treasury account, which is an easy access, high interest account that plays your money on the international money markets. Accustomed to them saying no to me, it was a rather pleasant surprise to actually have them say yes. Having noticed that our account was £200k in the black he asked if I fancied having lunch. I could not think of anything worse. We had got here in spite of our bank and I would never forget the episode with the credit card facility. I made a mental note that when we had our first million on deposit we would switch banks.

On Friday the salaries were paid. My daughter, Olivia, was born on the Sunday. She was beautiful and from that point on my world revolved on a different axis. It was the best weekend of my life.

But it was all about to go downhill.

CHAPTER SEVEN

A crash course in marketing

Marketing speak. It's when marketing people take a relatively uncomplicated concept and make it sound more complicated. You take a statement that's quite straightforward and you phrase it in a way that makes it sound far more important and clever than it actually is. It tends to be used by averagely intelligent people who like to feel superior.

So where I would 'do' a campaign, a marketing person would 'execute' a campaign. Also marketing people love to turn everything into a TLA (Three Letter Acronym) and any conversation is peppered with largely indecipherable and unnecessary jargon – meaningless if you're not in the business. So you'll find yourself talking to someone with a degree in communication and papier mâché from the University of South Staines about *executing simultaneous test strategies so as to maximize ROI*, which actually means finding out what works so you can earn your cash back and make a bit more on top.

Irritating jargon aside I was about to get a crash course in consumer marketing. While we had decided to keep the news of our investment quiet from the media community to enable us to continue to pay our writers and contributors a pittance, word had obviously slipped out and the guys from M&C Saatchi were on the door within the week. They had courted us before we had the funding, stating that we were a brand that they really identified with. Then, when they realized we were skint they went silent. Now we had money they were back sniffing around again. I wasn't sure

we should be using such a highfalutin outfit for our marketing. I know we had money but when you deal with players
in this league you can blow £200k on swanky lunches. We
pitched up at their offices in Soho Square and it was clear
we were dealing with the kings of the marketing jungle.
Everything was white. All the girls there were outstandingly
beautiful. I thought that there must be some sort of recruitment directive that only allows pretty girls to be employed.
I quite liked that. The place felt like it was 100 years in the
future and was the antithesis of our squat-like office accommodation.

I sat through a long and slightly boring meeting where our
brand values were explained back to us; their view was that
we should turn our back on our quaint line drawing ads
that had worked so well for us and do some more zippy and
unconventional design creatives. We took on board their
advice but when I explained that I was worried about the
high fees they calmed me by saying that we were not to
worry: they had agreement from the top that we could have
them on a monthly retainer, which would work out very
cost effective in the long run when we considered that they
were the top creative agency on the planet. The Saatchi
brothers, Charles and Maurice, were obviously famous beyond the media circles that I now inhabited. Charles is not
only the art-collecting husband of Nigella Lawson but, with
their first firm Saatchi & Saatchi, the brothers won award
after award and were hugely influential in bringing Marga-
ret Thatcher to power in 1979 with the slogan 'Labour isn't

working'. In 1995 they lost control of their business and set up M&C Saatchi in competition with their previously owned firm. Although I never came close to meeting either of the duo I admit I was dazzled by working with such a prestigious firm, and this was the first mistake I made. I lost sight of my costs and, from a business plan perspective, I went off piste.

We agreed a spend of £3k a month. Plus VAT. However, we should have continued to follow our instinct and design our adverts in-house using the resources we already had. It would take a disastrous campaign and a few months for me to fully realize what a big error this was.

By now it was early August and we had decided to postpone our first campaign with the new money until late September. I took a week off to spend it with Katharine and our new child and prepare for four months of solid graft as we built up to Christmas, which we hoped would be our big campaign. It was a strange time. After the euphoria of getting the funding and becoming a dad, the reality of being at home with a noisy baby that crapped and cried was rather stifling. It's not really terribly fashionable to admit it these days but I was just itching to get back to work and get stuck into everything. My mind was swimming with ideas and jobs that needed to be done. I knew an acquaintance who had also recently had a baby who started to leave his office at 5.30pm on the dot and never had a beer after work as he loved to get home and bath his new baby. What's that all about? At the time of writing nearly six years have passed since my daughter was born and four since my son, and children are without doubt the greatest thing that has ever happened to me. But the first six months of having an infant in your life is pure, mind-numbing hell. There is often talk in Britain of adopting a more continental style of parenting, with the fathers also getting six months paid leave to help raise their kids. I think the reason it never gets beyond a murmur is most fathers don't want six months off to look after a baby! It was a relief when my one week enforced purgatory leave was over and I could get back to the office.

After the break I met up with an another advertising agency recommended by the Saatchi people called All Response Media. Now if you're not involved in the advertising game you probably think that advertising execs are simply a bunch of coke-snorting, Armani-wearing tossers who drive around in Porches talking bollocks. And you would be right to think that as it's often true. However, there are two different sorts of coke-snorting, Armani-wearing, Porche-driving tossers. Firstly, you have the creatives – the sensitive souls who probably went to art college, who come up with the clever ideas – and then you have the buyers – the people who decide where the advert goes. The latter group are different to the creatives in that they do the deals and talk about money and are more likely to sell their granny. However, I got the distinct impression when dealing with *anyone* in advertising that if you wanted to buy a granny, and they had one still alive, most of them would do you a deal if the money was in the right ballpark. The phrase *ballpark* is used a lot in marketing too. So it's normal for a company that does a lot of advertising to have two agencies and, in most cases, the client will work with both of them simultaneously to run a campaign. It gets more complicated though.

Not only are there two different types of agency, there are also two different types of advertising. Brand advertising is where you try to get a message across to a large audience. The plan is for you, as a brand, to get into the lives and thoughts of the consumer so that, for instance, when faced with 15 types of beer at Tescos you subconsciously pick Fosters. You don't choose it because the packaging is blue, or it's 80p a can, or it's 4.5 per cent alcohol, or it's purported to be as Aussie as a Bondi Beach bum (even though it's brewed in Reading). You buy it because for some reason you identify with it. You buy it because you see yourself as a cool, young, confident guy, who likes girls and surfing and beaches and you have a wry, clever, slightly knowing sense of humour. You're different to people who drink real ale who have beards, large tummys and talk about plough-man's lunches and lack your sophistication, and you're different to people who drink Stella who like to punch you because you looked at them, kick in a shop window on the way home and then fall asleep in a pool of their own urine. Consumers are bombarded with thousands of advertising propositions every single day, so to get into the consumer psyche and get that person to identify with you and be loyal to your brand, your message has to be loud, clear and usually very clever. Some companies have become so successful at this that they change their business model so that all they do is marketing. Nike, for example, do not make shoes. They have outsourced the manufacture of their merchandise to companies all over the world who make their shoes for them. The bods in the Nike office concern themselves solely with the objective of making you a slave to their brand so that all you want to buy are their products. They have become a highly focused and very, very effective marketing machine.

The second type of advertising is Direct Response Advertising. This method of advertising is self explanatory. You place an advert somewhere and you expect to get an immediate response from that advert. If your knees are going and at night you have trouble getting up the stairs, you go and pick up a copy of *Old Fogey* magazine, look in the classified section in the back and, hey presto, a raft of ads for stairlifts. As a stairlift manufacturer you're after a very small section of the community, namely, old people in two-storey houses who have a lot of disposable income. Now, as a percentage of the population, people in the market for stairlifts are very few, so you target your advertising to that very specific niche market, as there is no need to turn the whole world onto your product. This second sort of advertising also appeals to small start-ups because few of us can afford the millions of pounds it takes to effectively roll out a national brand advertising campaign. DR was the route we were taking, hence our meeting with the guys at All Response Media. And they were brilliant. If the creatives were the airy fairy ideas people, the buyers were pure scientists. You almost expect them to be wearing white coats.

Liam Cronin was our point man at the agency and I had spoken to him a few days before our meeting. Liam had asked me to email over a copy of our database as he was going to profile the names and addresses so he could identify very specifically who our readers were. The postcodes of all our 10,000 readers were fed into a computer. These were then matched with postcodes on a master file. The data on this master file is phenomenal. It tells you the age of the person, annual income, how many holidays, how many cars, pets, toasters and any other amount of frightening information you would never expect someone to hold on you. Every time you fill out a warranty card for a new sandwich maker your data is collected and compiled and added. Liam had profiled our database and was about to drop a very large bombshell.

Sally, our marketing director, had just had her baby and was mostly working from home as her husband also had a full time job as TV exec. She had come up to London for the day having left her kids with her mother so that we could have a meeting, go and meet Liam and find out what his thoughts were on our prospective campaign.

Liam spoke in a soft, lilting Irish accent and Sally and I sat comfortably while his presentation washed over us. It was all interesting stuff and we were all in agreement that our reader was a well-heeled, well-educated, retired professional male who took five holidays a year, had a black Labrador, a Volvo and two toasters. We knew all this from our anecdotal evidence and from the number of people that rang Pauline to talk about the war and how the youth of today should be conscripted. Or hung. The presentation tripped along nicely until a phrase made me sit bolt upright in my chair.

'Using the data we think the potential universe for this product is about 70,000 people.'

'Wait, wait. What was that?' I said.

'Your potential universe is 70,000 people,' repeated Liam, patiently.

'Er, what the heck is a universe?' I continued, hoping it wasn't what I thought it was.

'It's the total potential market we think your product will appeal to,' said Liam.

'Really!' I was slightly taken aback by this news. I was hoping he would say a few million.

Now 70,000 is a lot of people if they are sitting in your back garden, but as a potential audience for a nationally available publication this was worryingly small. This is because in any market you can only hope to get a very small percentage of the total marketplace actually putting dosh in your till. If we were really good and managed to find and switch on 20 per cent of our potential market then we could expect to get 14,000 subscribers. This might be enough to eke out a living but it wasn't going to make us millionaires. However, 20 per cent is an astronomically high rate to achieve and it was likely to be in the low single figures. This blow meant that if we kept on the same course then this business was going to be in trouble. The alternative would be to broaden the appeal of the magazine and thus increase the potential universe. Although, in hindsight, I can now see that broadening the appeal of a subscription magazine is difficult – primarily because you market it to a specific audience. First, we would have to change the content. Then, when that was comfortable and you were confident you would not lose your existing readers, you could try a new marketing tack to try to bring in new people.

It was a worrying lesson and something that I should have thought about before. As a first time business owner I should have seen what my market share could have been rather than rushing in just because I thought the idea was a good one. Richard Branson is known for looking at all his prospective ventures from the perspective of total downside. I had only looked at the upside and by doing so had ignored a potentially huge flaw in our business. Branson would have done some preliminary research and asked someone like Liam what the market was like. Since that time I have often floated ideas past Liam to gauge reaction and potential market. You have to be more discriminating when it comes to a new venture and it's a lesson I will always take with me in anything I do.

Sally was working with the Saatchi people to get the campaign creative ready and Liam drew up a schedule of places we should advertise. This included the classified sections of the broadsheets, which we had previously done, but we were also going to test a whole load of new publications including *Saga Magazine* and a golf magazine. Liam's people had taken our client profile and matched that with magazines that also had readers of a similar profile. It was interesting that a reasonable percentage of our readers were also golfers. We also planned to do some direct mail by renting a mailing list which belonged to a company who specialized in erectile dysfunction products. Liam and Sally's modus operandi was to test everything. If it worked keep doing it like crazy until it stopped working. If it didn't work, obviously stop doing it immediately. Everything needed to have a unique response code so that we could measure each activity individually. At the time we thought it was the best strategy and we booked up nearly a half of our investment based on this course of action. If all the tests failed we would be in very big trouble, but the events of the past few weeks made us all confident that luck would be on our side.

With the marketing campaign pushed back, it looked as if August was going to be a quiet month and the magazine production schedule continued apace.

Now, spanking. I've mentioned this before and I was alarmed at quite how often we were asked if we could supply films of people being spanked. Spanking seems funny somehow and we laugh at it. There's something so very old school British about spanking someone and it throws up all sorts of visions of the country lord giving his servant a good thrashing. It's big business. There are clubs in London where a high court judge or leading politician can rock up and get trodden on and whipped all night. And pay for the privilege.

In the UK as a consenting adult you can be a spanker or a spankee as much as you like. It's a free country after all. But it's not possible for you to actually buy a film of people spanking each other. That's right. It's perfectly acceptable to watch a woman get screwed up the bottom by a couple of builders but if they give her a spanking it's illegal. And here's why.

In 1982 the British Board of Film Classification overhauled the ratings of films. What used to be an X was changed to 18 and R18. R18 was restricted viewing and was for films that showed people actually engaging in sexual activity without a flowerpot in the way. You could see everything and they showed those lovely close-up squelching shots that porn fans so love. These films were only allowed to be shown in places with a specific licence so you couldn't simply pop into your local video store and choose at will – in fact you couldn't buy them legally at all. This meant that people continued to purchase their filthy porn under the counter from all sorts of dodgy geezers wearing raincoats with poor levels of personal hygiene. Given there was a huge demand for this material this lead to criminalizing a lot of people who really weren't criminals at all. Also the measures that had been put in place to ensure that there was no bad stuff going on were pretty much ignored by the under-the-counter suppliers, so this illegal general porn was lumped in with all sorts of other nasty and violent stuff like paedophilia and snuff (films where people actually die on screen, although it has to be said I have never met anyone who has ever seen such a thing and it may well be an urban myth). It also meant that a perfectly decent middle-class banking sort of chap had to go and rub shoulders with a backstreet gangster to get something that really wasn't that bad. So, in the late 1990s, this problem was addressed and licences were made available to shops to sell R18 to the general public. However, the R18 guidelines for content remained unchanged. The category allows to show explicit scenes of consenting sex between adults. This is what is *not* acceptable:

- Any material which is in breach of the criminal law, including material judged to be obscene (this presumably explains why there are no porn films with a bank robbing plot).

- Material (including dialogue) likely to encourage an interest in sexually abusive activity (paedophilia, incest, rape) which may include adults role-playing as non-adults.

- The portrayal of any sexual activity which involves lack of consent (whether real or simulated). Any form of physical restraint.

- The infliction of pain or physical harm, real or (in a sexual context) simulated.

- Any sexual threats, humiliation or abuse which does not form part of a clearly consenting role-playing game.

So you see a film of someone being spanked contravened a number of the big R18 no-nos. However, there was clearly a demand and not only were people continually calling us to see if they could get them, but European film producers – who weren't much bothered about what the British film censors thought – were posting us samples to review in our magazine. The global nature of business meant that a company overseas could legitimately send whatever material they liked by post as the regulations only affected UK businesses. The internet enabled people to circumnavigate the entire regulatory system completely and many companies simply set up shop in Holland and posted their unregulated films to the UK clients, and there was nothing the authorities could do to stop it.

I decided to take one of these spanking films home and see what all the fuss was about.

I had clearly by this point become extremely blasé about the whole sex industry because on an early summer evening my wife was in the kitchen preparing our supper, our infant child was cooing in the bassinet at her side, and I was in the lounge, cold beer in hand, as I flicked on a Czechoslovakian spanking film. This bizarre scene of domestic bliss was only interrupted when my younger brother, Andrew, popped around for an unannounced cup of tea.

'Mate, I've got to tell you that this is odd,' he said.

'What do you mean?' I replied, keeping my eyes on the whacking about to take place on the screen. 'This is totally work related, there's got to be money in this spanking malarkey,' I continued.

And with that he grabbed a beer and settled into watching the film with me.

The odd thing about this genre of film is that there is no penetrative sex and apart from some topless scenes it's not even really that rude. It's just rather strange. I wasn't entirely sure what was being said as it was in Czech but there was a man in a suit who was pretending to be angry with the female protagonist. With much stoicism our heroine bent over a desk wearing stockings, suspender and a basque, and was given six of the best. The man held a wooden implement that was a cross between a table tennis bat and a cricket bat and he repeatedly laid into the poor girl's bottom. It wasn't a massive hard whack, more a series of slaps, but the accumulative effect left her bottom scarlet red and, if I remember my school days correctly, it probably hurt a bit when she sat down. I was completely bemused why people were so obsessed with this sort of stuff. It generally amounted to hurting people and although not disturbing it really wasn't in the slightest bit arousing. Perhaps it appealed to people who had been to boarding school and had been ritually beaten. I couldn't manage to get into the psyche of who would enjoy this but it did make me sit up and think about how much money could be made through providing things that they may find appealing. We had a captive audience of about 10,000 men who had a couple of quid and liked reading our fruity magazine. It was our duty to flog them stuff.

This is the Richard Branson philosophy. You create a brand like Virgin which people identify with. It's cool, it's got a cool boss with a beard and long hair, it takes a contradictory path to most other companies and it has high-profile, corporate punch-ups with established brands. It's a rebel brand. You take that brand, with its core value and existing customer base, and then you flog them a load of other stuff. So Virgin started off as a music mail-order business, then became a record retailer, then a record label. So you have millions of customers who think the Virgin brand is great. Then you sell them tickets on your airline. Brilliant. Then you sell them cola and weddings and telecommunication services and train travel and TV and then you create your own bank to put their money in. You can go from the cradle to the grave and, at every step, tip money into the Virgin coffers. It is pure genius and the interesting thing is that they don't necessarily own each company outright. In many instances they take a stake in a business that does something they think their brand devotees will buy stuff from and then they stick a Virgin badge on the front. I thought we would have a crack at this philosophy in our very own small way.

I wrote down all the things I thought our readers would like to buy from us.

- Zimmer frames

- Walking sticks

- Erection pills

- Stairlifts

- Dirty films

- Dirty books

- Whisky

Aware of my past brushes with illegal trading practices I avoided getting into selling erection pills on the basis that I was not a licensed pharmacist. Zimmer frames and walking sticks would be fairly small sellers so I put them to the bottom of the list. Stairlifts required quite specialist skills but the last three were ripe for sticking the *Erotic Review* brand on the front, and we got to work immediately in setting up distribution channels.

I was a busy chap and although we had funds in the bank I didn't want to go and spend lots of time and money sourcing all these products, putting them in a warehouse and then mucking about with posting them out. No, the sensible way to do this was to outsource it and then get paid a percentage on what sold.

I had recently had a meeting with a very enterprising woman called Stephanie Taylor who runs a successful mail-order business in the North East called Passion8.com. Stephanie had been selling vibrators and lingerie for years and was one of the pioneers of the sex toy revolution. She had come to see me to talk about doing some business together and to also tell me about a new website she had developed which would sell 18 certificate adult films. These were not the R18 films which could not be sold over the internet due to licensing restrictions. However, 18 certificate films could be sold without a license and it was with these films that we decided to go into business together. We would promote the films under the banner of 'The *ER* Film Club', Stephanie would arrange to take money off the client and ship out the goods from her warehouse. We would get 25 per cent of the price. Which could be about £4 a film. Not bad when you consider we didn't really have to do anything other than devote a page to the film club.

We also did a similar deal with a company selling books, and another that specialized in selling whisky. The clever part was that in each issue we would not only give each of the services a full page promotion, we would also review a book or a film, and then at the bottom of the review we could direct the reader to purchase the item via the website we had set up.

July and August flew by. Rowan kept the pressure up to get the magazine out on time and we recruited a new member of staff to reinforce the editorial team. We put an advert in the *Guardian* media section which comes out every Monday.

We had one response. Fortunately the respondent fit the bill perfectly and we offered her the job on the spot.

Susanna Forrest joined our troop. Exceedingly bright, a talented writer, a lethal sense of humour and great fun, Suzy slotted into the *Erotic Review* team perfectly, and with Pauline selling the adverts and looking after the Poshtotty girls the magazine was now fully operational. The team now consisted of eight employed staff: myself, Rowan, Annie, Susanna, Chris, Pauline, Sally and Michael. Plus, we had the designer Will on a contract for £1500 an issue which turned out at £15k a year, effectively another salary. We now had a headcount of nine people. We had come a long way since that rainy night in the Academy.

By September our big advertising campaign was primed and ready to go. Since launching the business I always tried to plan my future cash flow a few months in advance. You can have a four year business plan with a projected cash flow but I liked to look at it in a more short-term quarterly detail so I could really feel how the business was running. I ran a spreadsheet cashbook which told me what money had come in and gone out and I could see my up-to-the-minute cash balance. This spreadsheet always tallied with the current bank balance so I felt I had a handle on exactly how much money I had to the penny. I also ran this forward into the future anticipating when big bills were due such as the payroll and printing bills. I also put in my anticipated cash receipts so I could plan how and when I was going to pay the smaller suppliers, and one thing that struck me very quickly and with significant alarm was how we had managed to spend a large chunk of our investment on not actually doing anything. It's amazing how much money nine people and an office will actually drain when there is nothing coming in. When we had banked the investment we also paid off a load of old debts, and now we were spending a monthly payment on the Saatchi contract. We had actually spent £30k, which was above what the business plan had predicted. We had assumed an investment in July and an immediate launch of a marketing campaign would generate cash almost immediately. By delaying our campaign we had sat there and spent our money and not created any income, we had not made the money work for us. It was my second big error and, by not asking for more investment at the time we got it, I did not allow myself any room for mistakes. The only way I could make up the difference was to cross my fingers and hope that the advertising campaigns did better than we expected. All Response Media called and said they needed £50k in their account to spend on the marketing campaign and by the beginning of September our account was down to about £120k. It was about to get much worse.

CHAPTER EIGHT

Cracks appear and things are not going to plan

I t is said that a butterfly can beat its wings in Hong Kong and cause a hurricane in Texas. The butterfly effect: small, seemingly insignificant occurrences that can have large repercussions. For example, who would have known that a little blue pill would be responsible for wiping out a long-established and very specialist trade, its practitioners thrown callously to the winds. Since the dawn of the porn era workers known as fluffers were diligently plying their trade in the adult movie business. The fluffer's job was to keep a male porn actor aroused by oral and manual stimulation. A porn shoot can go on for hours and it can be tiring for the actors and sometimes the male star will lose interest. So, a fluffer is charged with keeping him standing to attention and ready for action at all times. It was an important role in the porn world and never in their wildest dreams did they think that their trade would simply cease to exist overnight. That fluffing would stop.

Then some scientists working for Pfizer trying to find a cure for high blood pressure accidentally discovered the enhancing effects of consuming small amounts of Sildenafil Citrate. Or Viagra as it became known. Viagra changed the world. It reintroduced sex to pensioners, it gave worn-out men back their confidence, it put the zest back into tired relationships. In some instances it ruined relationships when a quite happily sexually inactive late-middle-aged wife was suddenly presented with a husband behaving like a randy seventeen year old. And it obliterated the prospects of a whole industry. The fluffers found themselves out of work and not really fit for anything else. It is believed many of them found alternative careers in estate agency.

In my own way I had discovered the butterfly effect, and the apparently small act of postponing our marketing activities by a couple of months had resulted in a worrying large hole in my cash flow. The business plan predicted that by this stage we would already be investing the income we had made from our non-existent July campaign. We had planned to roll the subscription income forward as it came in and spend it on more marketing. By now we should have been on the second roll. The knock-on effect meant that I was about £40k behind where I thought I should be at this moment. I decided to put it to the back of my mind and forge ahead with all the other exciting stuff we were working on.

Rowan had embraced broadening out the readership of the magazine and had managed to bag an interview with the *uber* cool artist Tracey Emin in the October issue, which came out in late September. This was trumped by the November issue which had interviews with celebrity chef Anthony Bourdain, famous philosopher AC Grayling and rock star Nick Cave. As a small niche publication we were really punching well above our weight in talking to famous people and the magazine started to get quite a buzz about it in London media circles. Rowan was popping up on TV all over the place and we had hundreds of thousands of pounds worth of free publicity through TV, newspaper and radio interviews.

Roberta, our PR partner on Poshtotty, rang to tell me that the *FHM* issue due out at the end of September was going to feature our Poshtotty photo shoot and, on the day it went live, I sat eagerly with our web designer crossing our fingers. On the first day of the magazine's release we had about fifty people sign up, and it was great to see the beginnings of some revenue from our idea. It was the first time that I had actually come up with a fresh concept and turned it into a cash-generative business model. It has to be said though, that I was rather hoping for around 1000 sign ups to plug my cash flow gap, and the results were rather disappointing given that a whopping 700,000 men read *FHM*. But it was early days and the magazine was on sale for a month.

We had held off putting up new Poshtotty girls on the site until the promotion went live, and now that it was, and people were paying good cash for the privilege of seeing naked posh ladies, we were obliged to put up a new set of pictures each week. We had about four weeks left before we ran out of Poshtotty girls altogether which meant that another photo shoot had to be arranged. Quickly.

We ran another advert in *The Stage* and Pauline started interviewing the girls. Triggers and I had a chat about getting a load of shoots done over a few days so that we could build up a bank of images and we wouldn't have to do it again for a while. Seeing some money coming in made us all even more enthused about the project.

We decided on a two-pronged strategy. We would do another big location shoot and also spend a couple of days going out in the car doing individual shots of girls in their own surroundings. For some reason we had a whole slew of girls who lived in Essex. Essex girls are famed, incorrectly in my opinion, for their lack of intelligence and loose morals.

Q How do you know when an Essex girl's had an orgasm?

A She drops her bag of chips.

That's not nice, is it?

Fifty per cent of the respondents to our adverts came from Essex and there did seem to be a common trait amongst them, although it's not the one given to them by the media or stand-up comedians. The overwhelming characteristic of young Essex girls is an absolute charming naivety. We were bombarded by applications from girls who genuinely believed they had the looks to be a model. And for whom that would never happen. This blinding, mass-collective misconception is entirely down to an utterly reprehensible type of business that has flourished over the years, specializing in developing modelling portfolios for young and gullible girls.

Here's how it works.

- You are a girl in your late teens with little in the way of academic success.

- You work in a shoe shop in Lakeside.

- You watch *X Factor* and dream of being famous. All the time.

- Your dad says you are beautiful and that you are his little princess. Your Nan tells you that you have a lovely singing voice. They are wrong.

- Your friend at work tells you about this modelling agency that is looking for talent.

- The modelling agency offers you a free photo shoot.

- You go to the agency and they make you up like a tart and take photos of you.

- You don't get the pictures though. If you want the pictures you have to sign up to their portfolio programme. You have to pay to get the portfolio put together (which amounts to half a dozen pictures) and they tell you that they will start to promote you to the big modelling agencies. Before you know it the smooth-talking sales person has relieved you of a grand. You use your holiday fund, sacrificing that cherished fortnight in Magaluf, thinking that you are investing in your future fame where life will be one big holiday and you could even *buy* your own apartment in Magaluf. You walk out with your pictures under your arm and you never hear from them again. Your dad, furious at your treatment, rings them up to demand your money back and they refer him to the small print and, in particular, clause 4c.

Clause 4c. We don't actually have to do anything and in all likeliness will not lift a finger.

Everybody knows of Andy Warhol's oft-quoted and chronically overused view on our allotted 15 minutes of fame. That is now redundant. Reality TV has distorted a whole generation's view on what they can aspire to. Fifteen minutes of fame is nothing, they want fame forever, for whatever. The portfolio services, the prophets of false hope, feed like leeches off this desire to be 'someone'. The sheer volume of applications we received – with the hallmark, heavily done-up 'professional' shots – represents what can only be a vast ocean of people living with disappointment, and dreams that will never come true. People always criticize the producers of the pop star shows for being so callous to the singers who audition in front of them. I agree with what they do. If you can abruptly dispel the idea that you might be famous, no matter how brutally, then it opens the door for that dreamer working in a shoe shop to get on with throwing themselves into the footwear game with gusto. And I'm not being condescending either. They might not be the next Madonna but they may – unknown to them at this moment in time – be a retail genius who could one day be the next Anita Roddick or Philip Green. Living with the misconception that you have singing or modelling talent and are moments away from being spotted can put your entire youth on hold and stifle other talents that you might have. It can literally ruin a life. I've seen first-hand the damage that false hope can bring. It's an epidemic.

We needed women with the right look and the ability to act grandiose and, in essence, we were looking for actresses rather than porn stars or glamour models, or eighteen-year-old kids who had been ripped off. Out of the volumes of applications, we managed to find a few, but I felt sad for the girls we rejected. And the sense of fun that this project had started with was waning as I saw myself getting closer to an industry I wanted no part of. Even the unsolicited naked shots in my inbox each day were becoming annoying, vast files that took an age to download only to reveal some hapless young girl with rugby player legs in a cheap thong trying to look coy. I never wanted to exploit people and it became clear that although we were not engaged in explicit porn I had put myself in a position where I was using someone's need for cash to do something they might not be entirely happy doing. What next? Should I open a sweatshop in Brick Lane? Or a salt mine?

Nevertheless, there was a commitment to the customers who had paid good cash for our service and to the Poshtotty team, and we needed the money to plug my cash flow gap. So we forged on.

Triggers and I planned our day on the road and jumped in the car destined for Essex. As well as being cheaper than hiring a location, we also thought this might provide more varied backdrops and scenarios. Although the site was predominantly amusing I wanted to make it look like we had lots of ladies living all over the country rather than doing shoots all in the same property. A keen observer would have noticed that the first ten shoots were all done in the same overly stylized Mile End house.

Kate was an experienced lingerie model and we turned up at her house in Barking bright and early at 10 a.m. She lived out of town in a modern estate and no matter how we tried to shoot we couldn't make it feel posh enough. There was a dearth of poshness on this side of Barking. Even the garden was a barren yard, which lacked merit as a backdrop, so Kate suggested we go down to the woods and perhaps do some outside shots. Kate had a friend with her called Kirsty who, understandably, she had asked to come along just in case we were a couple of nutters. I was aware only when we turned up how dodgy this whole scenario could be. A couple of strange blokes put an ad in *The Stage* and then rock up at your house in a crappy Saab to take some fruity photos of you getting your kit off. It sounded like a lurid crime story in the papers. Kate suggested that she and Kirsty drive to the woods in their car and we follow in ours. As we drove, Triggers and I started to feel nervous. What if *they* were a couple of psychopathic loonies who were going to lure us to a shack in the woods and chop us up with concealed axes? We laughed about how amusing this whole scene was; all four of us driving into the unknown, slightly nervous of each other. About half a mile from the house, their car pulled off the road and down a dirt track into a beautiful little spinney with a brook bubbling through the middle. The sunlight cut in through the trees and there was that comforting damp smell of a woodland with autumn just approaching. I remember thinking how charming this was, and snapping out of it when I realized what it was we were doing. We had asked Kate to dress posh, but she has misunderstood us entirely and was dressed like a cheap hooker in a tight black boob tube, a pair of stockings and some red high heels which sank into mud as she tottered along. It looked odd with the backdrop of the spinney, but it appealed to my sense of the absurd and we found a little bridge which was perfect to shoot on. In the absence of studio lights – and Triggers being a consummate pro – I had to kneel down out of shot and reflect light back up at Kate while she did her thing. Triggers wasn't some point-and-shoot amateur; everything had to be lit properly. Absorbed in the necessity of getting a good shoot quickly and efficiently, I was fairly immune to girls stripping off and Kate wasn't in the slightest bit embarrassed about doing it. She strutted around on the bridge and it was shaping up to be a brilliant session until a wet, heavily panting black Labrador bounded over the bridge followed by its shocked owner. We all looked at each other, forced into each other's personal space by the narrow width of the bridge.

'Morning', said Triggers, ever polite as if we were out on a nature ramble.

'Er, yes, morning', replied Mr Dogwalker, looking down, avoiding eye contact, avoiding looking at Kate in underwear, stockings and red high heels.

Nothing more was said. Nothing could be said to explain why four people, one of them in their underwear, were standing on a bridge in a spinney in the middle of Essex.

After the shoot we walked back to the car pleased that our first outdoor venture had gone so splendidly.

'You didn't even get to see my pierced clit,' said Kate, disappointedly.

'Yes, we don't really go in for those kind of shots' I replied.

'Shame', concluded Kate. Triggers raised an eyebrow at me and did not need to say anything. We weren't quite as used to this stuff as we thought we were. I handed Kate the usual £100 fee and we said so long and went to our separate cars.

And that would have been that except as I was putting my key in the ignition Kate came running over.

'Kirsty has asked if she can do a shoot.' Seeing Kate make such an easy hundred quid, Kirsty had obviously decided she might as well have a go.

This was a great opportunity. For £100 I could get another Poshtotty girl bagged and we could probably do the whole thing in 20 minutes.

'But she doesn't want to take all her kit off', continued Kate.

'Fine,' I replied, 'but we only pay £50 for an underwear shot.' I was getting cannier about this by the minute.

I was keen on these underwear only shots as I could use them for publicity and £50 was a bargain. Kirsty was prettier than Kate. She was not a model and had a more curvy natural figure. I wanted the Poshtotty girls to be real. Accessible. This was supposed to be part of the charm and Kirsty was a warmer person, and had a touch of class. In many ways she was a better Poshtotty than her chum. And at half the price. These little victories in life.

To the right of the cars was an open field of wheat stubble that rose up gradually to a small hill, and I had the perfect idea of what I wanted.

'OK, team, this is what I want this time. Think *The Sound of Music*. Kirsty, you're Julie Andrews skipping around the Alps.' I was warming to my theme, replacing the sun-drenched mountains of Austria with a stubbly wheat field in Essex. 'I want you to run up that hill shedding clothes every 20 seconds, Triggers you're running behind, Kate you've got to follow Triggers, keep out of sight and use the reflector as he instructs you.'

The three of them sped up the hill to the sound of the camera shutter and as they reached the brow of a hill, Kirsty clad just in white cotton undies waving her shirt above her head, they came face to face with a yellow tractor.

'What the fuck are you doing?' yelled the driver.

Back at the office I looked through the photos. Despite untimely interruptions from dog walkers and farmers it had been a productive day. We had managed to bag five sets of shots, it had only cost us £450 and would keep us going for another month. Pauline was planning another big shoot for early November and we had managed to hire a farm for the whole day for £200. We would try to do ten sets which should keep us going until Christmas.

Sally was now ready for the launch of our new press campaign, which it was scheduled to kick off on a Sunday in mid September. We had adverts in *The Sunday Times*, *Independent on Sunday*, and *Telegraph*. We wanted the *Daily Mail* but they would not let us advertise as they thought our ads were too smutty. It was a nerve-racking weekend because not only did I need the campaign to come in as we had forecast, but I really wanted it to do about fifty per cent better to make up for the unexpected losses we had made in the past two months.

We came in on the Monday morning and it took until lunch time to get the results.

They were bad.

We had done about 30 per cent of our expected business. This was devastating news. We had a whole raft of other campaigns going live over the next six weeks which could make up the difference, but I was keenly aware that I had no contingency budget in place should the other advertising campaigns under-perform as well. If everything we did came in less than our forecast assumptions, we would go out of business by the following summer. After the euphoria of the past few months, where failure was never really considered, I was face to face with the reality that we were on a knife-edge. The next six weeks were going to be crucial as to whether we survived or failed. Failure, the real F word, loomed on a hitherto cloudless horizon.

Rowan and I had our first management meeting with The Boys in early October. Mr Big and his partner took us to a very exclusive club called Marks. Marks is a club for the people who run the country. Its members are the cream of society and it was terrifying, not least because jacket and tie were required to get in. Since my stint in the art world I took a very laid-back attitude to my dress. Usually I wore a pair of jeans and brown trainers. If I was meeting someone I might put on a nice pair of brogues and a shirt, but I very rarely wore a suit. I had one in the office on the back of my door should I have to go and meet The Boys or someone important, as I did that day. But, as is the fashion these days, I never wore a tie. Ties are for weddings and funerals. The Boys were always impeccably turned out, and it was embarrassing to have to be shown down to a basement by one of the porters where I was fitted with a tie before going up to lunch.

There was a note of disbelief that we had managed to spend so much cash so quickly with such poor results, and what had previously been a jovial encounter with The Boys was tainted with concern. It didn't stop us drinking four bottles of wine and a few G&Ts, and we drifted back to the office late in the afternoon still feeling confident although less bullish than we had been before. Obviously it was not game over but, as chief executive, I had a huge responsibility to protect their investment and I didn't take this lightly. I had to do my best to make up the shortfall, and I started to look around at other things we could do to make a couple of quid.

The video and book clubs were trundling along but weren't making huge profits. The whisky club was a complete disaster and we didn't bother doing it again. We were making anything up to a thousand a month from the first two which was better than nothing, but it wasn't enough to make a substantial difference to our downward trajectory. Something needed to be done to get us back on track. Like an adult sex fair.

It was at this point that I met one of the most interesting people that I came across during the entire episode. Savvas Christodoulou. Savvas runs an exhibition called Erotica, which he started from scratch back in the mid 1990s. People describe this show in a myriad of ways. If you are open-minded, you'll think it's a place for liberated people to express their sexuality and do a bit of business. If you are a prude and don't like that sort of thing, you would probably call it a perverts' car boot sale inhabited by the spawn of Satan. It's a mixture of both. During a weekend in November 80,000 people flock to Olympia to visit the exhibition. Three hundred stand holders are waiting to sell their sex-related wares. You can pretty much buy anything you want, from hardcore porn to edible body paint, to a fully kitted out dungeon, to a shaver designed to be used on your pubic hair (if you get carried away you can buy a pubic wig called a merkin, incidentally). You can find crotchless pants, strap-ons, 1000 different types of vibrator, thigh-high, red patent leather boots, whips, piercing and rings of every nature, tattooists, corsets made from materials ranging from barbed wire to rubber, sellers of erotic book, artists and photographers of every style. You can even book yourself a summer holiday to a French chateau where you can swap wives for the week. My immediate thought on this was that I bet it cuts out any holiday bickering or arguments about map reading. In amongst all this you have transvestites, gays, lesbians, fetishists, exhibitionists, straight couples, invalids, old men wearing dirty raincoats with jock straps underneath, young girls wearing bikinis, pissed gangs of lads buying their year's supply of porn, models, wannabe models, nymphomaniacs, marketing executives, press and radio reporters, entrepreneurs, investors, Germans, wholesalers, retailers, accountants, deal-makers of every hue, perverts, voyeurs and people who want to come and just hang out and be in such eclectic company. It is an amazing experience. A place where prejudices are left at the door and where anything goes. Outside the doors of Olympia, genteel Kensington continues about its business oblivious to the three day carnival of depravity and lust that rages inside.

Savvas has built the business where so many have failed through sheer force of character. He is a hard man to bargain with and comes from the Genghis Khan school of business. If you're on his side he expects you to stay on his side. If you ever betray him then he would most probably have you boiled. He owns half of Romford and to own anything in Romford you need to be reasonably hard. But he is no gangster. He is of Greek ancestry, there is no doubt in that, but the really unnerving thing about him is that as well as being hard he is a chartered accountant and sharp as a piercing needle. So there is absolutely no bullshitting this man. However, the staccato exchanges with him always make me think I'm in a scene from *The Godfather* and I'm about to meet a sticky end:

Phone rings 6 p.m. I am at home.

Gavin: 'Hello?'

Savvas: 'You are not my friend.'

Gavin: 'Er, hello?'

Savvas: 'I said you are not my friend. I thought you were my friend, Gavin. But now I think you are not my friend.'

Gavin: 'Oh, hi Savvas, er what the…?'

Savvas: 'I have heard there is a new adult exhibition opening in Brighton.'

Gavin: 'Yes …'

Savvas: 'I have heard you are involved. This means you not my friend.'

Gavin: 'But, but, but, all I did was send down some magazines to be given out at the door. I'm hardly "involved". Honestly. Really. I promise.'

Savvas: 'You are either with them or with me. I thought you were my friend.'

And so it continues until we establish that I have not disrespected or betrayed him and he does not have to have me disposed of in a shallow grave somewhere.

But, despite the Godfatheresque conversations we have, he is one of the most straightforward and impressive people

I have met since I went into business. I think we're friends. If you find yourself in London in late November I would recommend going to Erotica as it's insane.

Savvas offered me a subsidized stand on the basis that we would advertise the show in our magazine and encourage our retired officers to come down and spend some money. This was a perfect opportunity to make an extra couple of quid and I jumped at the chance. I had an idea to sell subscriptions on the stand at £20 a go. As an incentive I would give away a free gift at the show. A show special they call it in the trade. I talked to Dai, the Welsh fireman, to see if there were any really cheap sex toy gadget things we could give away but the only thing he had was a painful looking set of anal love beads that you could shove up your bottom. It looked unappealing and I decided to look elsewhere for a deal that might tickle the fancy of a prospective subscriber without them having to risk rectal trauma. The trick here was to buy lots of something that had a high perceived value but actually cost next to nothing. As usual my friend Jamie from over the hall at EPS came to the rescue and offered us a hardbacked book that he was having trouble shifting. It was no surprise really as it was crap. It consisted of about 200 pages of pictures of naked women taken with a Polaroid. However, it was a hardback, and weighty, and on the back it was priced at £20. This meant I could sell a subscription at £20 and give away a free book worth £20. From a consumer perspective I thought this was a bargain and I bit his hand off. I bought 1000 at 50p a pop. I paid him his £500 and we designed some free-standing posters to take with us to make the stand look more exciting.

The show itself was unbelievable. Sally, Annie and I manned the stand over the weekend and we were absolutely gobsmacked by what we saw. It was a freak show. It was wonderful. I'll never forget seeing a 70-year-old man in a leather coat being led on a dog chain by his 70-year-old wife who wore an ill fitting oversized leather corset, her sagging breasts clearly visible through the sides as she slowly walked along dragging him behind. Although a very amusing and unusual sight I was happy that such a place existed that they could freely indulge their fantasies like this and once again I looked back on the strange trajectory that my life had taken over the past few years. Erotica was not the answer to our cash-flow problems and we sold only 200 subscriptions over the weekend. This injected four grand into the coffers but it also left me with 800 worthless but very heavy books that I had to lug back to the office. I broke the lift by overloading it, trying to get them up to the fifth floor, which was a miserable end to a disappointing show. I had to carry them up ten flights of stairs. It took me a whole morning and made me hot and tired. Furthermore, Jamie refused to buy back the unsold copies so they sat in my office gathering dust reminding me daily of yet another hasty deal turned duff. Genghis would not have put up with this. He would have burnt them along with a handful of treacherous low-life spies right there on the pavement on Regent Street. And he would have nailed Jamie to a tree.

By the end of November the rest of our campaigns were in full flow and, one by one, they came in under the target. We were generating income, so we had stopped simply spending the investment, but because the cash was coming in significantly less than expected, it paid for the running of the business only and did not leave a surplus to reinvest in more marketing activities. Without being able to take that surplus and spend it on getting more customers, the business would slowly strangle itself and eventually go under. It might take six months, but I could see that we did not have nearly enough money invested in the business to make it work as we had predicted. Also, at the back of my mind, I had another niggling feeling that I had been suppressing since the meeting with Liam back in the summer. Was our marketing not working because there was not actually a demand for the magazine? Had we simply got behind an idea that we liked without considering if there really was a viable market out there? Was this a dog with fleas? Perhaps there WERE only 70,000 people interested in what we had to offer, plus a bunch of fans at the Academy Club who cheered us along because they liked Rowan. Perhaps people liked their porn straightforward and dirty and our proposition for classy, educated, erudite, well-written erotica was good on paper but, in practice, people wanted filth. Plain and simple filth.

The reality was that in October and November we had forecast acquiring about 12,000 new subscribers, each paying £25. We had anticipated £300,000 worth of income based on our investment plan. This money was supposed to be reinvested immediately into acquiring yet more subscribers. It looked like our total income was going to be about £50,000 which was way short of the mark. Our business plan had predicted we were supposed to spend about £200,000 on promotion in the last quarter but, so far, we had only spent £60,000 because the rest of the money was not there. And finally here was the truth: *we had spent more getting our subscribers in the door than what we actually made from them in revenue.* The enormity of our miscalculation slammed home.

I suddenly became very frightened indeed.

Despite the shortfall and the bleak outlook I tried my best to remain positive. Poshtotty was actually kicking in some money now and this was not even in the business plan. I thought that the best thing was to get behind this and try to think creatively about new revenue streams that didn't require a massive outlay. I even thought in the darkest moments that we could actually close the entire magazine, make everyone redundant and just run Poshtotty. If we sunk the rest of our investment into this venture it had the potential to make £10,000 to £20,000 a month, and it would pay Rowan and I some money and also slowly pay back the investment to The Boys. But, in the cold light of day, I could not see how anyone would agree to this. Rowan's passion was her magazine after all. It was hers and she had put every ounce of herself into it. I think The Boys were in it because of the lure of owning part of what could be a famous magazine – and the idea of owning a slightly amusing and fruity website as a substitute was not one that would have turned them on. Also I wanted it to work for the team, and felt I owed it to Annie, Pauline, Sally and Suzy to do my best to pull it around. Chris by this point had become quite sullen and wasn't really playing as a team member. I think that working with Rowan was quite a frustrating exercise for him, as the whole editorial side was run on a crazy timescale. The production schedule was a rolling programme of deadlines and, in most publishing companies, the work is spread out evenly throughout the month. So when a magazine goes to press the editorial team breathe a sigh of relief and then start working on the next one. They commission the written work, get it in from the writer (on time), edit it so it's the correct word count and sounds right, find some pictures or photography or commission an artist to illustrate it, then get the words proofed so there are no spelling mistakes. Then all this raw material goes to a designer who puts it all together and it's proofed one final time as its laid out on the screen so that all the indices match and the pictures fit the words with the right credits. Finally the adverts are dropped in around the finished article. The designer then converts the whole thing into a specialist electronic file and this is sent to the printer who turns it into magazines. And then the whole process starts again. Each of these stages has a deadline and people feed into the operation at the appropriate time.

With our schedule, Rowan usually spent the first two weeks away from the office working on other writing assignments, courting celebs and going to cool parties. Then all the usual magazine activity was jammed into the last two weeks when it should have taken four. The team would work through the night, the most intensive hours, to get the magazine done in time so that the next month's schedule was not mucked up. It was always an unnecessarily arduous process and it invariably led to mistakes but it had always been that way. My view was that so long as the deadlines were met, it was not really my concern as to how Rowan ran her editorial team. Annie and Suzy had only ever worked for Rowan so knew no different, and they were incredibly loyal but sometimes I could sense the pressure they were being put under. Chris, on the other hand, had worked for a number of publishers and found this method of operating slightly challenging. Furthermore, I don't think he ever really warmed to me, and probably thought that I was just some chancer trying to make a quick killing. In many ways he was right. I had no real desire to run the *Erotic Review* forever and never developed the passion for it that the editorial team had. From a business perspective I wanted it to make a profit and use it as a launch pad to either move on to more lucrative magazine concepts or sell my share for a profit at the first possible opportunity. However, rather than confront the issues, Chris became miserable and withdrawn and when things started to get hard I became disillusioned about him too. I had risked my house to get this venture going and I thought it reasonable to have the team on side. I figured if he was not happy why didn't he go and work somewhere else? I often wish we had talked to each other about it because neither of us are bad people. Indeed, I always had great admiration for his writing and thought he was a fascinating guy. The resentment festered and it should not have been allowed to.

Pauline meanwhile had gone off on a slightly crazy tangent. While she was excellent running the Poshtotty recruitment and selling the adverts she was also involved in doing her own review section called Pauline's Private Views. In this section, Pauline went off around London to various art exhibitions and shows that had a sexual or adult theme. I had been invited to these things from time to time but in the adult business I am described as 'vanilla'. This means that I'm pretty much straight down the middle and don't go for being tied up, or sharing Mrs G with a bodybuilder on a holiday in France. In truth, I'm fairly prudish and, even though I am more broadminded after my Poshtotty experiences, I like to go home after a hard days work and have some supper with the wife, maybe a nice glass of red wine and chat about our respective days. We'll watch a bit of telly, hopefully a nice ant documentary narrated by David Attenborough, and then go to bed. Without a pair of handcuffs. What I don't like doing after work is dressing up in a leather gimp suit with the bottom cut out and going out to watch someone in a cage having custard thrown at them. But London is a large and varied city and Pauline started to get more invites to dungeon parties and fetish events and, before I knew it, she was running with a quite racy crew. I'm not saying that Pauline was up to no good; she was after all happily married. It was just amusing seeing someone who I thought fairly straight going to these strange events and embracing them with such fervour.

Pauline became friendly with the Sheridans who ran a fetish club in a converted arch in London Bridge. Brian Sheridan is a force of nature and is fond of telling everyone how beautiful his wife is and how much money he has banked. His wife, Caroline, is very sweet but terrifying. She always reminds me of a curvy Joan Collins and is a very sexy lady. There is something about a mid-forties predatory female that scares me to death. Pauline and I took them for lunch at the Academy, and they were telling me all about their adventures while running these fetish club nights. Brian could see my obvious discomfort at the regaling of such tales of depravity and said, 'I think you need to take your foot off the gas with Gavin, dear.'

Caroline winked at me with a heavily-mascaraed eye and purred. I gulped. She would eat me alive.

They are an extremely entertaining couple and I can't imagine a dull moment in their company. Brian had purchased the club from a crackpot robot inventor. This inventor had made a pile of money out of robotics and had developed a night club concept. He had acquired a railway arch under London Bridge Station and, at significant cost, clad the whole interior, walls, floor, ceilings, bar, toilets in aluminium. In one corner there was a robotic aluminium barman and lots of buttons with the names of cocktails on them. You simply pressed the buttons and the robot sprung into life and made you your chosen cocktail. The only problem was the robot inventor chap knew more about robots than how to market a nightclub. So without promoting it, or visits from Jordan wearing a bikini made out of string, the aluminium-clad night club remained unknown and unvisited and the robot barman was unused and unloved and seldom made cocktails. So the robot inventor put it up for sale. Seeing a good deal, Brian purchased the club lock stock and barrel and turned it into a sort of fetish/free love/robot party night where, in the privacy of the basement, you could dress up in a rubber German WWII uniform and fumble around in dark corners with lots of strangers. It felt a bit like a space ship, and the whole place clunked as you walked round. Brian brought energy and flair and more importantly his whole fetish crowd to the club and the robot barman sprung into life, pleased to be useful. Once established in their new club, Brian set about applying for a licence so that he could allow people to have sex legally on the premises and, on the face of it, everyone was happy. That is, apart from the people running Southwark Cathedral which for 800 years had been pretty well respected in the area and was located very close to the club. The Dean of the Cathedral lodged an objection to all this terrible fornication on his doorstep, claiming it was like Sodom and Gomorrah, and called down fire and brimstone on the heads of the sacrilegious Sheridans. He had met his match with Brian and Caroline (who enjoy the soubriquets of The General and Lady Caroline when partying at the club) and a full-on media spat ran through all the London papers. At one point the Dean was accused by the Sheridans of sending three private detectives along to their New Year's Eve bash dressed as The Three Musketeers. Like I said, never a dull moment with the Sheridans – and Pauline, their new best friend, was in the eye of the storm.

In amongst Brian securing himself a place in hell he also rang me one afternoon to tell me that his wife was a brilliant writer. I told him to send something in. A few days later we received a 1000 word fantasy interspersed with not very subtle plugs for their club and ranges of jewellery.

'I'm not publishing THAT', said Rowan.

'Fine, I was just passing it on', I said defensively. I didn't much care whether it went in or not. 'But if it's not good enough you can tell them.' I didn't fancy telling Brian that Rowan didn't like the way his wife wrote. You don't want to get on the wrong side of these people.

Rowan delicately told Brian that it wasn't really an editorial fit and I thought that was the end of it. The next day the phone rings and Brian is on the other end.

'Gavin, my good man', he announces.

'Hi Brian, how are you?', I respond.

'Tell me, if I take out an advert how much is a double page spread?'

'It's about £1500', I reply.

'Excellent. I'll book that please.'

And with that he sends through the designed advert. Except it's not an advert. It's the story that his wife had sent in. We accepted the ad and Rowan made sure there was a big banner on the top that said ADVERT to assure readers that this was not an article commissioned by her. You have to give it to Brian. He always gets what he wants.

It was a strange time in London and not only because of robotic fetish clubs. The anti-war movement had gained huge popularity and there had been massive protests in the capital, the likes of which had never been seen. Rowan had been on the march and was all riled up about it and the December/January double issue was a 'Make Love Not War' special, dedicated to the magazine's anti-war stance. At the time I was quite pro war but kept quiet as the rest of the team seemed quite agitated about the topic. It seemed to me that if there is a tin pot dictator wandering around doing what he liked and gassing his own people, then blowing him and his criminal family to pieces and giving the people of that country a shot at democracy was a good idea. I was wrong. Turns out I was wrong about quite a few things in 2002.

The only problem with hiring a farm in November to shoot posh ladies taking their clothes off is that it's really cold.

We had the farm down in Kent booked and we had been given free rein on the place for only £200. The farmer, a friend of Triggers, had also let us use the mobile horse-box which had a very horsey-smelling lounge with a blow heater that kept the temperature slightly above the nipple chilling 5°C it was outside. I was ferrying the girls from Sevenoaks station in my clapped out Saab, Pauline was giving them warm oxtail soup in the horse truck trying to stave off hypothermia, and Triggers was striding around in his wellies with his hound, completely in his element. Roberta, our PR, was there looking a million dollars in her city gear and trying not to stand in the various types of animal shit that littered the farmyard. The tech guy turned up too and helped make tea, crack jokes and generally keep spirits up. It was like a scene from Scott's tent in the Antarctic. Pauline would stick her head around the door of the horse truck and say, 'OK, next'. We would all look at each other huddled around the blower. Reluctantly, a girl would get up and open the door as a cold blast of air came in.

It was the usual procedure, except it was colder and muddier and nobody was really having a good time. The girls earned their £100 each that day, I can tell you. We had them mucking out stables – naked, riding horses – naked, fixing a tractor – naked. We also did a remake of my *Sound of Music* idea and Triggers ran around a field chasing a naked beautiful French girl. There were two farmhands who could honestly not believe their luck that day.

The whole thing was fairly miserable and we finally ran out of natural light at 3.30 pm when we did a shoot of one of the girls getting her kit off in a hay barn. It was freezing and we all shivered as we nailed the final shot. Knackered, we all drove back to London and got together in the pub to talk about the day.

'There has to be a bloody easier way to get these shots', I said, ' these are killing me.'

'I agree,' said Triggers, who was by now getting a bit cheesed off with the paltry share he was getting. He could earn a lot more doing a dog and did not have to spend a day getting embarrassed talking about genital piercing.

'Well, I love it', said Pauline, characteristically.

'You could always buy in stock', suggested the tech man.

'Eh?' I said. 'You can get this as stock?'

Magazines and newspapers run on stock photography. When you read an article on telecoms and there's a picture of a young handsome jet-setting sort of guy in a suit using a mobile phone, that image is not actually shot for that magazine. What happens is the picture editor working on that magazine will ring up one of the big stock libraries and say 'I'm looking for a young handsome jet-setting sort of guy in a suit using a mobile phone' and the chap from the stock library will send over several examples, your picture editor chooses one, a price is agreed and no need to send an expensive photographer out to find the right picture. You can get your photos for as low as £30 a go. If you look carefully and have a good memory it's possible from time to time to see the same images being used in different articles. I never in my wildest dreams considered that such a thing as porn stock photography existed. I was wrong. Of course the porn industry is as advanced as any other.

This was a revelation. The tech guy showed me a few websites that could supply whole sets of pictures of girls stripping off and although they were never going to be as quirky or as amusing as the ones we had shot ourselves it was still going to save us a lot of time and a lot of money. Many of them were probably Eastern European but I didn't see this being a barrier and besides, we could buy each set for about $50. This was about the quarter of the price we had previously paid, plus we didn't have to leave the comfort of our own office and spend time haring around Essex in the winter upsetting farmers. At a slash Pauline lost her job as casting expert and Triggers was made redundant. Neither minded that much and we came to a fiscal arrangement with Triggers that worked out his day rate for the work done to date so there were no hard feelings. It had been fun, but it had been hard work with little reward. Triggers had a steady income anyway and Pauline could spend more time on flogging advertising space which, although hard, was one way we could make an immediate difference to our monthly bottom line.

Despite the savings I had made on Poshtotty I was pessimistic about the future. I kept trying to add on revenue streams but they were just too small to make a material difference. The chatlines were doing alright and we were selling mucky films and books at a reasonable rate. I also purchased a load of faux leather binders with the *Erotic Review* badge on. These were used to keep the collection of magazines together, and we purchased them for £5 each and sold them for £19.99 plus p&p. It was a nice little earner and we sold a couple of hundred. But again it wasn't enough to stem the tide. We were sinking, and I didn't know what to do.

It was now Christmas and all our marketing campaigns had fallen short. We had our Christmas party in the Academy and I felt slightly removed from it. I couldn't bring myself to feel happy about our current situation and I left the office and took a couple of weeks off with the rest of the world – to celebrate the birth of our saviour by eating too much fatty food and buying crap that people don't want. I used the time to try to think about what to do next. We had about 90 grand left in the bank and I had started delaying payment of non-essential bills. I knew that my friendly bank would never give me an overdraft and it was clear that in the new year I would need some breathing space. The cheapest way to get an overdraft is not to pay anyone for a while. You effectively use your suppliers as your overdraft facility. It's cheaper and, although creditors moan about not being paid, they don't take your house as a personal guarantee. It's not an ideal position, but I thought we might need a load more money to keep going and this could take six months to obtain. Michael shared my outlook and vowed to have a good think over the break and come back in January and hit the ground running.

I went home to my wife and daughter who was beautiful and by this time had started smiling and looking at me. I wondered what I was going to do. These two were the most important people in my life and I couldn't let them down. I had to provide for them come what may.

CHAPTER NINE

The wheels come off

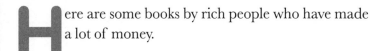

Here are some books by rich people who have made a lot of money.

- *Anyone Can Do It* – Duncan Bannatyne

- *Anyone Can Do It* – Sahar & Bobby Hashimi

- *Screw It, Let's Do It* – Richard Branson

- *How to Get Rich* – Felix Dennis

- *Make Your First Million* – Martin Webb

- *How to be Really Rich* – Peter Jones

- *I was raised in a small cave and I conquered the Eurasian land mass. And it was really easy* – G Khan

Felix Dennis is one of my all time heroes but what makes these people want to proclaim how easy it is to do it? Felix is a smart ruthless guy; I've met him as you will find out in due course. Not everyone is like him and I simply don't believe his path to great wealth was easy. I'm sure it's the same with the others. Do they know it's not easy and want to rub our noses in it? Shouldn't their books be called *I Combined Luck with Obsessive Hard Work and Total Ruthlessness to Make my Fortune.* Doesn't have the same ring to it.

Anyway, as you can see from my story so far you will realize it's hard. And at this point it was manifestly clear to me that the *Erotic Review* was unlikely to be the venture that was going to make me my million and the Porsche before I was 40.

Instead of coming back in January, after the Christmas break, feeling recharged, I felt only dread. I knew that before me was the unenviable slog of finding a new investor or a buyer and it made me despondent. In only six months I had come from being on top of the world to feeling like a failure and it was hard to pull myself out of the hole.

Sally rang to say that All Response Media needed another £20k to roll out the Valentine's Day promotion. I knew this was going to be difficult with our ever decreasing reserves but decided to go for it. We could sit there and not spend anything and prolong the death or go out with a bang, so I agreed to spend the money on the campaigns. I knew that Genghis would have gone into battle, sabre rattling, all out for glory rather than hide away in his yurt waiting for the end. Go out with a bang, not a whimper I thought to myself.

January and February crept by and the Valentine's campaign was disappointing as expected. It wasn't that the advertising didn't work, it was simply that we had overestimated the effectiveness of the campaigns we ran and the amount they would bring in. We had based our results on the response we had got when we launched back in February the previous year, but looking back on that period the magazine had been unpublished for six months and the publicity around Rowan and I purchasing it had obviously given us a tremendous tailwind. We simply had not accounted for a diminished response and we had made no provision in our cash flow forecasts for this. Put simply, we did not raise enough money even to have a shot at making it. By March, the money was running out fast and I started to feel I was losing grip on the situation.

Michael had stepped back from the business a little as there was not really a requirement for a full-time finance guy and we saved money by not having him there. I was raising the invoices and looking after the cash book and Michael and I got together every couple of weeks to review things. At one of our regular meetings he realized shortly after walking in that all was not well and he took me to a new steak restaurant to give me a pep talk. I knew he was concerned as he only ever had lunch with me in greasy spoons – anything more than a full English breakfast (including tea & toast) for a fiver was outright profligacy in his book.

'OK, the wheels are coming off but you have to step back from it', was how he started his uncharacteristically wordy pitch. He continued. 'Your job now is to look at this as a project that needs completing. Your job is to find a buyer for the *Erotic Review* so that it does not go bust. After you have done that you can find another project. Do not take this personally, do not get emotionally involved, it is just a

project. Deal with the project. Complete the project …'
This went on for the length of time it took to order and eat
a steak and fries and, by the time our lunch was over, I was
a new man. OK, I might have been brainwashed slightly
as he didn't let up for an hour but it did the trick. I took the
Michael Carter patented 'helicopter view' and stood back
from the problem, viewing it from 8,000 feet. It seemed less
problematic from up there, away from the angry contributors and suppliers and the pressure from the investors.

It was what I needed. I had allowed myself to get too personally wrapped up in the failure of the business and it
hadn't even failed yet. I had to up my tempo, get myself excited, get pumped. I would never be able to find a solution
if I felt sorry for myself, nor would I be able to get anyone to
buy into the business if they thought I didn't believe in it or
feel confident about it. My sole job now was to stop trying
to build the business up with lots of small revenue streams
and concentrate on selling the company. This would enable the staff to keep their jobs, Rowan to continue to run
her magazine, The Boys to protect their investment and
I wouldn't have to go through the indignity of going bust
and failing so quickly after telling everyone how successful
we were going to be. I left the restaurant and took a deep
breath. That pep talk has stayed with me and carried me
through many years and a few tough situations and I tend
to look at business now as a series of projects. It doesn't
mean I care any less but it helps me deal with it better now
that I approach things as if they are not going to result in

the end of the world. I always put a brave and enthusiastic face on – no matter how bad things get. One thing I learnt from that time was that if you can motivate yourself and be positive then others around you will be positive which, in turn, makes you even more positive.

So I knew what I had to do. If I stretched the payments out maybe we had six months left. Michael encouraged me to call a board meeting where we presented the facts to The Boys. We thought it was important to have a session where we outlined where we were and what options we had available rather then spring it on them when we had 50p in the bank some time in late May.

The company was losing 10 to 20k a month. Although The Boys had hinted that they might be prepared to put in a little more money it was clear that to create the financial space to enable us to make the *Erotic Review* a viable business there would be a requirement of £250k. They were not interested in this proposition mainly because they were understandably worried that in another six months we might be back in the same situation.

Carrying on regardless and pretending that everything was OK was out of the question as, by the summer, it would be game over.

So the options available to us were as follows:

- Share overhead

- Find significant new investor(s)

- Sell the business

- Go fundraising as a PLC

The share overhead option. This meant finding someone to partner with – for instance, a magazine of a similar size and turnover. This would enable the two publications to merge offices and management and share the infrastructure costs. This was an unlikely option because we sat between two stools. Few mainstream magazines would want to get into bed with something as rude as the *Erotic Review*. On the other hand, porn mags would not want to team up as we simply weren't filthy enough. Plus the porn magazine industry was very quickly being wiped out by the internet as a cheap and private way to view explicit adult material so there were few players left in this magazine sector.

Finding significant new investors. It was clear that we had underestimated how much money was needed to market the magazine. If we could find another £250k then we might be able to turn it around. The problem with this was that new investment would dilute my shares and I really didn't want to go on working for a firm that I had created where I was a minority shareholder. It would feel too much like a job. I had given it my best shot and it was now time for someone else to have a go.

Selling the business. This was the best option as far as I was concerned. It would present me with a clean exit and might even provide me with some cash with which to start another hare-brained scheme. The magazine could run more cost efficiently within another publishing group drawing off the central operation.

Go funding as a PLC. Michael put this on the list as he really wanted to run a PLC. I think this was more of an interesting project for him rather than a viable way of saving the business. We had done all the preliminary work but I wasn't too keen on this idea now for the same reasons as finding another investor. The PLC route would be costly and we needed a lot of money up front to make it happen. We would have to risk a large chunk of our cash reserves just to get this scheme of the ground and if it didn't work then we would go bust straight away.

No, the option that worked for me was to sell up, and we agreed that this was the best route to proceed down. Rowan, Sally and I also agreed that we would come off the payroll. We had less than £30k in the bank and we needed to keep the business going while a buyer was found. I had some savings so I knew I could meet the mortgage but it put a burden on the three of us not only trying to save the business but also personally not bringing any cash in.

Savvas was running an erotic exhibition in Manchester and had promised to give me a stand in return for advertising which I had run in the previous two magazines. When the time came I could see no valid reason to actually do this. I knew from talking to friends I had made at Olympia that the northern version only pulled in a quarter of the visitors of the London show and by the time I made the posters, driven up the motorway with Annie and Sally with our crappy books and paid the hotel bills for three days we would actually lose money. However, it seemed such a waste to turn away the offer of a stand that would have cost us a couple of grand and since I had stopped taking a salary out of the business I was short of cash so I decided to do a bit of wheeler-dealing on the side to make a couple of quid. So I rang a friend of mine called Mike Carroll who ran a very successful website called Blissbox.com. I told him that I had a free stand at Manchester and that it might be fun to spend the weekend up there flogging rabbit vibrators. If we could use his stock at wholesale prices I would provide the stand and we could split any money we made 50/50 at the end of the weekend. He knew a couple of promotions girls who were used to doing these sorts of things so we crammed his car and my car with the girls and as many vibrators as we could fit in. We got in nearly 1000 of the things and headed off to Manchester. We stayed in the Midland Hotel (although being a bit mean we put the promo girls up in a twin room in the Travelodge about half a mile away), which is a big posh hotel opposite the Gmex Centre where the exhibition was taking place. We piled the rabbits up under the table we had rented on the stand and I had got six posters done of a cute little bunny and we blue-tacked them to the back wall. Nil points for design.

We were like a couple of Del Boys for the weekend. We flogged them for £20 each and they flew out the door. Our pockets were bulging with cash and although it was three really hard days of solid graft it was a fantastic experience. This is what business was about. Flogging stuff, pockets full of cash and gallons of beer at the end of each night. It was great fun and we walked away after all the expenses with five grand cash each and a weekend to remember.

Now, how to go about selling a business?

If you have a company that is a market leader in selling widgets, the chances are at some point someone will make an offer for it. At the time of writing there is lots of international money looking for a place to invest and this money finds its way into the city. Traders and dealers in the city in turn look for businesses that lead the market and throw off money and invest this money in them. You might routinely use a product or service that ultimately is part owned by the Sultan of Brunei.

Similarly, one of your competitors – or someone in a similar sector with a bulging bank account – might see the acquisition of a business in the same field as a quick route to achieving increased market share.

So, any business that has a good track record and a rosy future will attract attention either directly from investors or indirectly from a company doing a similar thing to you.

If you are the market leader and it's your business you might well not want to sell of course. It's fun running a business that makes money and that has happy employees who know what they are doing. Why sell when you have worked hard and it pays you a good wage? And anyway, you might want to buy your competitors and grow your own business into a multinational conglomerate. Successful businesses get offers all the time and the owner has the luxury of saying yes or no.

Unsuccessful businesses are more tricky to sell however. Principally because, as a failed business, you have demonstrably proven that your business model doesn't really work, and potential buyers don't like businesses that don't work. It really is not what they are about. However, there are certain pitches you can make that overcome this obvious shortcoming and draw their attention to other points that might not be immediately obvious:

1   The business model might be sound, it's just that it has been underfunded. With investment it can be scaled up and eventually become very profitable.

2   The idea may be sound but the cost of overheads make it unviable. Any company not profitable on paper might be profitable if you move it into a

business where the infrastructure is already there. So, rather than a stand-alone business it becomes a department slotted into an organization, which means you can instantly cut out certain overheads such as the managing director, finance director, rent, accounts people, support staff etc. – plus you can make economies of scale on the items you purchase for the business. In magazine terms a publisher with 30 magazines will be able to buy paper significantly cheaper than a magazine publisher with just one title.

So, it was clear that the best route for selling the *Erotic Review* was going to be another publishing company. Now, how to value the business.

A business can only really be valued on what someone is prepared to pay for it. So, during the first dotcom bubble, corporations acquired internet start-ups for astronomical prices that were later proven to be worthless. We were not a dotcom business so it was unlikely that I was going to be able to walk away a millionaire. Certain industries have standard ways of assessing how to attach a value to a company. During our fundraising activities the previous summer I had learned about the valuation of publishing businesses and I was now able to put this into practice. Magazine valuations are generally done in two ways: either through multiplying the turnover by a factor or multiplying the profit by a factor. It usually works out at one to two times turnover or five to ten times profit. Obviously this can be more if someone really wants a magazine that is on the up.

The mantra I learned during my first year of running my own business was 'turnover is vanity, profit is sanity'. However if we were going to pitch the idea to another company we would ignore the lack of profit bit and concentrate on highlighting the turnover, which had increased throughout the year. If costs could be stripped out of that, as I explained above, then the person buying it could possibly turn it into a little goldmine.

Obviously we could not sell it for a multiple of profit since we hadn't actually made a profit. So we wouldn't talk about that. We reckoned we had turned over about £300k in the last financial year so we decided this would be the value. It was actually quite a nice valuation if we could get it because it would a) pay The Boys back their £100k leaving £200k and that would mean that my remaining 30 per cent would be £60k. I would have considered this a result of sorts given that I had put £25k in and drawn a salary for a year or so.

So Michael stepped back up to the plate and we drew up another business plan based on our past performance – with some assumptions based on the new information we had gained about growing the business. We decided to carefully target some key people in publishing houses that we thought might be interested in acquiring us. We had to think carefully as most mainstream publishers wouldn't touch us with a bargepole, but we came up with a shortlist and Rowan wrote the letters and we posted them off and waited.

So now we were trying to sell the company but I had to keep positive and work with Rowan to keep the magazine going and fend off the ever increasing tidal wave of creditors to whom we owed money. Poshtotty was now being filled up with shots of cheap Eastern European girls with dead eyes. It lost its appeal after we stopped doing our own shoots and controlling the creative side and, sensing the downturn in quality, Roberta drifted off and became less involved. Without her input the publicity dried up and it slowly stopped generating money of any significance. Although in the middle of what was quite a depressing episode our tech guy came up with the idea for Grottytotty which was our own send up of the site using stock photography of ugly naked girls. Yes, that's right, someone had set up a photo library of ugly naked girls. It was very tongue in cheek and we only charged a fiver to sign up. Incredibly people were paying to see this site so we continued to update it every week with a very ugly naked girl. The naked shots from models kept flooding into the office and we got to the point where we just put them in a pile on Pauline's desk. One day Pauline picked up the phone and I listened in to the one-sided conversation.

Pauline: 'Erotic Review, how can I help?'

Pauline: 'Yes, when did you send that photo in?'

Pauline: 'And your name is … ah, Janet, yes I have it here.'

[Pauline shuffles through the photos on her desk]

Pauline: 'Er, no, we're not going to use you for a shoot. You don't quite have the look, I'm afraid.'

Pauline: 'Yes, I'm really sorry.'

Pauline: 'However, we do have a new site called Grottytotty that you might like to be involved with.'

Pauline: 'OK, bye.'

[puts phone down]

Gavin: 'She wasn't interested, then?'

Pauline: 'No, she said that wasn't what she was looking for. I wonder why?'

Pauline had continued to look after me and provide me with moments of unintentional hilarity like the episode above. Only someone with complete honesty and lack of cynicism could offer a hopeful glamour model a contract on a site for ugly women over the phone. She genuinely thought she was helping. One concern I had about the sale was how Pauline would cope. Rowan and the team would fit into a new young media company and Chris by this stage had left and gone to work for a book publishing company, which provided him with sanity, respect and a regular pay cheque. But Pauline was different. I knew that media sales teams in big publishing firms are full of young crazies, shouting down the phone, high-fiving and trying to shag the receptionist on a Friday night in the pub. But Pauline was precious and, although good at sales, she only really functioned in this slightly odd, out-of-the-ordinary business. Mainstream media would probably not work for her. On selling the title I would of course include her in the staff roster – but how would she cope? The solution presented itself to me one day when Pauline came into my office later than me for the first time ever, looking very glum and without the breakfast treats or the beaming smile that had kept me going through some tough days.

She was leaving.

Leaving to go and sell ads for Tim Woodward who ran a fetish magazine called *Skin Two*. As I had mentioned, Pauline had been spending a significant amount of time with the London fetish crowd and this had seemingly resulted in a job offer to work for the undisputed fetish bible that is *Skin Two*. I didn't try to stop her and knew that Tim's operation was as bizarre as ours and that it would be a good career move in an odd sort of way. Pauline left that Friday into the arms of another publisher and my guardian angel was gone. It was the end of an era and I knew things would never be the same again. It was now time to really get stuck into selling the business.

We thought the best way to proceed with selling the magazine was for Rowan and I to do the initial pitch and then we could follow up with Michael who could talk about the numbers and contracts, which can be quite complex when selling a business, even one as small as ours.

Our first appointment was with the famous James Brown. He is a magazine genius who was editor of *Loaded* magazine which led the way for the lads mags in the 1990s. His latest vehicle, IFG Publishing (I Feel Good – James Brown, geddit?), had floated on the AIM stock exchange and we knew that they had money for launches and acquisitions. They had recently acquired *Viz* magazine and a small stable of other lesser known titles from John Brown Publishing. It wasn't a great meeting and I felt a certain arrogance towards us. I suppose he had no reason to be anything different as he is a famous and successful guy in magazine circles but I came away disappointed because I had been quite excited about meeting him – knowing that not only did he once have the job every young lad wanted but he was a spokesman for a generation. My generation. I later found out that they weren't in a position to acquire any more titles as their latest big launch, *Jack* magazine, had been a flop and had cost them a lot of money. I also discovered that despite the cool reception we had received they were in the same boat as us and were looking for a buyer. Everyone in business is putting on a front. As the economist George Soros famously said, 'you only find out who is wearing a bathing costume when the tide goes out'.

I came back to the office despondent; of the ten letters we had sent we had received only one reply and I was starting to panic that we might actually go bust. At my lowest ebb Susanna put through a lawyer to my phone extension.

Head in hands I picked it up.

Gavin: 'Hello.'

Tubby: 'Is that Mr Griffiths, the publisher of the *Erotic Review*?'

Gavin: [wishing I wasn't] 'Yes. It is I.'

Tubby: 'Mr Griffiths, I am a solicitor representing a client that wants to sue you.'

Gavin: 'Er, why?'

Tubby: 'Slander.'

Gavin: 'Slander?'

Tubby: 'Yes, slander. You recently wrote an article on the website Punternet and mentioned my client, Mandy. It is my opinion that you have slandered my client thus causing her to lose business. We wish you to either retract what you have said in writing or we will be pursuing damages through the courts.'

Explanation

Punternet.com is a website where a punter (the person visiting a prostitute) can review the performance of said lady of the night. It's like on Ebay – when you buy something you can rate the seller. Other punters can check up the reviews and thus avoid disappointment. Copyright prevents me from showing you a page but you can browse the site at your leisure. I was amazed at its existence and looking at it again couldn't drag myself away from the reviews but then the internet has ended up ranking everything else so why not sex? It did cross my mind how great it would be to have a site where the girls rated the punters. There isn't one.

One of our writers in a previous issue had suggested that it might be the case that not all the reviews were legitimate. He suggested that rather than an exchange of real information it might be that the girls themselves were writing their own reviews in order to increase business. Take Mandy, for example. He questioned that rather than a romantic, candlelit, rose-scented room with a sensual 21-year-old nymphet, the truth might well be a tired-looking, middle-aged woman answering the door in a grubby dressing gown and sex may be a disappointing few grunts on a dirty towel on a mattress in the corner before you're turfed out on the street £200 poorer and slightly bitter. It was a fairly cynical piece but it was well written, reasonably short and sweet and I had not really thought how Mandy would feel about it. Our circulation was sufficiently small that I always thought we were pretty much immune to slander.

Anyway back to Tubby.

Gavin: 'So, can you tell me the name of your client?'

Tubby: 'She goes by the name of Mandy.'

Gavin: 'Right, is that her real name?'

Tubby: 'No. That is her working name. She will not divulge her real name.'

Gavin: 'Right, can I have your name?'

Tubby: 'No. Let's just call me Tubby. I am a barrister in a London firm and I am one of Mandy's clients. Because of the sensitive nature of the subject I would quite like to remain anonymous. So Tubby, if you please.'

Gavin: 'So, let's get this straight. You use this prostitute. You are going to sue me but nobody is prepared to actually give their real name.'

Tubby: 'Well. Yes. But I was rather hoping that you would print a retraction before we were forced to take further steps.'

Gavin: 'Can I take your number?'

Tubby: 'No I'll call you in seven days to find out what your decision is, then we shall be taking action.'

I put the phone down incredulous. Normally I would have laughed but this was on top of all the other pressures of not having any money and with that somebody dropped a letter on my desk that had been sent by recorded delivery.

It was our top flight firm of accountants taking us to court for not paying them on time.

CHAPTER TEN

The final battle

Genghis Khan was born about 1165 in central Mongolia. His father was the leader of a small nomadic tribe but he was brutally murdered when Genghis was only a small boy. Internal rivalry within the tribe led to his mother and five younger siblings being abandoned in the harsh Mongolian wilderness and left to perish in temperatures that can drop to below minus 40°C. The early years were a struggle even to stay alive and it is said that during this time he killed his own brother for stealing food from the family. As a teenager he seized back his place as his father's rightful heir, killing those who had committed such treachery against his family. In 1206, still in his thirties, he conquered and united all the tribes of his country and became Emperor of Mongolia. In 1211 he invaded China, which resulted in one of the bloodiest battles in history, and made the emperor of the northern province kneel before him. He died in 1227 having never lost a battle and his sons went on to rule one of the largest empires the world has ever seen stretching from Hungary to Korea. He was an inspirational and ruthless leader but he was also a creative and innovative visionary. Today 1 in 200 people on the planet can claim descendancy from him. I consider him to be the ultimate self-made man.

I knew that it was time to go into battle. Surely if one man could change the face of the world in such a way then I could sell a small niche adult magazine. If we could just get in front of one of these publishers I was sure with our passion and energy we could do the deal.

We made a few other unsuccessful approaches to publishers and received less than encouraging feedback. A porn magazine outfit in Essex were briefly interested but backed out before we could turn up with our roadshow. We met a media entrepreneur who was starting an investment fund to launch several magazine titles but no matter how much I tried to persuade him he couldn't see the fit. It started to look like the curtain was coming down and I prepared myself for the worst. But there was a glimmer of hope when we got a call from Richard Desmond's right-hand man.

Richard Desmond is one of my heroes. Sure, he's got a bad reputation but like Genghis he has fought his way up from nothing. He left school at 14 and got a job on the *Thompson Directory* flogging classified ads. By the time he was 21 he owned a record shop and shortly after that moved into publishing music magazines. He first published *Penthouse* in the UK and then developed a raft of adult titles. Although wealthy by this time his really big break came when he published *OK* magazine in 1993. It was perfectly timed with the rise in celebrity culture and its success enabled him to buy the Express Group in 2000. There are many rumours circulating within the media world about his alleged underhand way of doing things but he doesn't care what anyone says. He has made it on his own terms and the guy is a legend. I was thrilled and excited at the prospect of meeting him but we had to make do with his number two.

We met in the *Express* building overlooking the Thames at Blackfriars. It was a tough meeting and it became clear that we were not going to get anything like the £300k we were looking for. They explained that if they paid £300k and then spent another £250k on development they might as well use their own £550k to start from scratch. We suggested that perhaps he acquire half the business and move it into his stable. We would keep shares in the company and be paid out in time as the magazine started to generate a profit.

He fixed his eyes on me, sensing my inexperience. 'We're not good at joint ventures,' he said. We were lambs to the slaughter. This sort of deal would have opened us up to being completely shafted and he was sparing us that. There was little chance of a deal being done here other than a fire sale to save my reputation and walk away with nothing.

We stopped off in a pub for a few drinks on the way back to go through our options. Rowan said that she would rather go bust than work for this company and I realized at that point that even if I wanted to give it to them to avoid the company folding Rowan would not let that happen. At our lowest ebb we walked back and I prepared myself to get Michael in and go about closing the business.

Just before Regent Street is a little side street called Kingly Street and we often cut through there to get back to our own little grungy office. As we walked back we saw a man get into a Rolls Royce and drive off.

'That's Felix Dennis,' whispered Rowan even though he was 100 yards off and well out of earshot.

It was a sign. We rushed back to the office and Rowan wrote one of her most flowery letters playing the full damsel-in-distress card. We got Annie to go round and post it through the door of his office.

Now, to this day, I do not know why Felix was not on our list of people to contact but he should have been our first because, in magazine terms, nobody does it better. Like Genghis and Richard Desmond he came from nowhere. His first title, *Oz* magazine, ended up with an indecency trial and him actually going to prison. On his release a few weeks later he was walking through the West End when he saw a Bruce Lee film being shown in Leicester Square. The UK had gone kung fu crazy so he immediately released a kung fu magazine. He went on to release computer magazines just ahead of the computer boom then he saw the lads' magazine market develop here and rushed straight over to America and launched one there before they caught on. *Maxim* was at one point the biggest selling magazine in the world and he owned it lock, stock and barrel. He has been slightly ahead of all the other publishers on every big trend over the past 30 years and I think he has a time machine.

Within a week of sending him the letter Rowan went to see him in his private office. I prayed that Rowan did to him what she did to me when we first met. I had been captivated by her enthusiasm and if she could get his interest and hook him I was confident that I could present a good business case for taking it on.

He liked what he had seen and a week after that initial meeting Rowan and I were sitting down with two of the great man's lieutenants. We picked the business plan apart in the first half an hour and we got the sense that they quite liked it. There were lots of further questions but it became clear that we were onto something and that we could have found our buyer. By now it was early June and we had actually ran out of money. We didn't have enough in the bank to print another issue and the creditors were getting really cross. This was nail-biting stuff but we had to keep our cool and pretend that all was well otherwise someone might get wind of our dire predicament and try to wind the business up and sell the assets to pay the debt. Or go into liquidation as it is commonly known. The liquidator will liquidate your assets, turn them into cash, and pay back the money to the creditors. Not that we really had any assets anyway. We had a manky sofa, some old computers and a magazine title that having been through two owners hadn't managed to make any money – ever!

Phase two was about to get significantly more difficult. Ian Leggett got involved. Ian is Felix's money man and is as hard as nails, great fun and brilliant company and we've met many times since those days, but it was very clear he did not want the *Erotic Review*. As the finance director he held the purse strings and he had no intention of paying £300k for, what was in his opinion, an underperforming magazine. We got the impression that the head man had said he wanted it so Ian's job was to play hardball and he laid it down fairly clearly what he wanted to pay. Nothing. However, he was prepared to let those with shares be diluted to 10% of the business so that if in the future it was a success then we could get something back.

Now this put me in a rather difficult position. By this point I had written off my £25k as a bad business decision and really just wanted to avoid the thing going bust on my watch. It was clear that his was the only option available to us but I could not let that be known.

I had the unenviable job of going back to The Boys and effectively telling them that the only choice for them was to give the magazine away apart from a few shares and they would lose all their money.

All this was taking place within a half mile patch of London. Michael and Rowan were in our office, Ian was in the office just off Regent Street and The Boys were down by Marble Arch, a nice stroll up to the end of Oxford Street. So I walked down to see them. I sat in the boardroom crapping myself. They came in glum faced and were unsurprisingly not very obliging because they were pretty much about to kiss goodbye to their investment. They said that they wanted the loan of £100k back and £50k for their shares and providing this was done they would be happy to take a bath on the other money. Keeping some shares back would enable them at least to make some money one day so it wasn't a total loss.

So I walked back up Oxford Street to see Ian Leggett again. He said he didn't want to pay much more than £50k of the loans and no money for the shares. I look back on that time and think about the game that was being played between all these people with me stuck in the middle. Firstly, there was Felix Dennis – worth nearly three quarters of a billion who wanted the title, then there were The Boys worth half a billion each and, in the middle was me, fighting for my reputation, being bounced like a little ping pong ball between them … up and down Oxford Street.

It had already been made clear from the beginning that I was not going with the rest of the team, that was part of my pitch – you roll the magazine into your business and you save management and office overhead cost, so there was not an awful lot in it for me other than to avoid having a bankrupt business on my hands. The Boys stuck rigid to what they would accept and Ian wouldn't budge from his offer. I was absolutely paralysed waiting for one of them to give.

Michael and I sat in the office and I paced up and down the carpet, wearing it thin, waiting for one of them to break. I needed something to take my mind off it so Michael taught me how to play poker and we divvied up the petty cash tin and gambled the proceeds between us. For two days solid I did nothing but play poker and wait for one of these multimillionaires to make a move.

Tubby rang. Wound like a coiled spring I lost it. 'Just fucking sue me!' I shouted at the phone and slammed it down. I never heard from him again and we never retracted our article.

It seems incredible now but we just kept going with the business. The day-to-day running of the magazine continued and only Rowan and I knew that we couldn't get another one out the door. We carried on trading, but we knew that it was a matter of days before we had to tell the truth.

Eventually there was a break. Ian rang to say that he had been thinking about it and could I go up to their main office on Cleveland Street to have a chat. I walked up and it rained heavily so my trousers and feet were wet when I arrived as I had only a small umbrella with me. Ian sat me down. He could see that all my hopes were pinned on him and he shook his head and said that it was off. He couldn't see how he could make it work but was prepared to sit down with Michael and I and talk it through one last time. Wet footed, rejected and dejected I walked from his office back to the flea pit. It was the lowest point.

Friday came and Michael and I went up to the Dennis Publishing boardroom. This was the last opportunity and we had to make this count. At the end of the long negotiation there was £25k difference between what The Boys wanted and what Dennis Publishing were prepared to do. We haggled until it was early evening and I rang Mr Big at home and told him that in my opinion this was as close as we would get to a deal that worked for both parties and that in two days we would have to close. There was no other company interested so this really was it. Seeing that we could go no further The Boys called back to say they would accept what was on offer and a few days later Dennis sent a team in to do due diligence.

I handed over the cheque books and the printers and salaries were paid at the end of the month. The magazine did not skip a beat and the readers knew nothing of the turmoil that had been going on behind the scenes for the last few months.

I was signing some of the sale papers in their office and Felix walked in. Here was my hero, a man I had always hoped to be able to meet on an equal level. Instead I felt small and insignificant. I was the opposite of him. He had made a fortune from magazines and my first one had lost me a pile of money. I felt like a failure.

However, there was one final piece of good fortune, albeit very small. As the deal was being finalized a little piece of information came to light. I had an employment contract which The Boys had insisted on having drawn up when they invested their money which tied me into a six-month contract. At this late stage they realized that to get rid of me

I would have to be made redundant and so I got a six-month tax free pay-off of £25k, which would be enough for me to take a few months off to regain my composure and decide what to do next. It also nicely matched the money I had put in at the beginning. The whole adventure, while far from being a huge success for me, had actually been cost neutral. I looked on it as 18 months of the most intensive business schooling at no cost.

The last issue to bear my name inside the front cover was the June 2003 issue and a very competent new publisher was put in place who took the reins of the business almost immediately. Pretty soon I was out of it. Rowan and the girls were moved into a little corner in the Dennis Publishing HQ and Sally was also laid off a few months after me. We never had a formal goodbye party, the magazine sailed on and eventually Rowan left a year or so later. At the time of writing it has been through three more owners (making six in total) and is currently owned by Jamie Maclean at the EPS. The man who started it all is now the seventh owner.

Poshtotty closed. Ownership of the site went over with the new owners but nobody at the new organization had the stomach to run a site that had become a showcase for Eastern European hookers and, without the amusing stories to back it up, its charm had gone. Grottytotty closed too. Which I think was a relief to mankind. Nothing good would have come of that. The tech guy moved to Gibraltar and became an internet millionaire.

The new company also offered me a three month consultancy to bed the magazine into the new business but in truth it took me less than a few days. Realizing that I was being paid for not actually doing anything I asked the MD if I could do anything else as I felt a bit guilty just taking their money. He had been quite keen on all my brand extension ideas and although they had not amounted to much with the *Erotic Review* if he did the same thing with his titles that sold many thousands more than our little rag it could have been a big revenue earner. I did the report and there was talk about me going to work with them as a consultant but it didn't ever come to anything. There was also a job going in international licensing and in a half-hearted way I went for the interview but didn't get it. I knew deep down that I didn't want to do this. In many ways I was frightened about starting from scratch again but knew that it was the only way for me now. I had a head full of ideas and I was free. More adventures were waiting around the corner and I went home to Katharine and Olivia to start working on my next scheme. It's what Genghis would have done.

First Guest: 'What do you do, Gavin?'

Gavin: 'I'm a failed magazine entrepreneur.'

First Guest: 'That's interesting, what happened?'

Gavin: 'Well …'

The story continues

The trouble with being bowled out the first time is it makes you rather apprehensive when you find yourself back at the crease again. First time around you're going to smack it for six and hang the consequences. You wind up the most almighty swing and the anticipated triumphant thwack of leather on willow is substituted by the horror of splintering bails and stumps exploding in kindling behind you. It's a lonely and shameful walk back to the club house and you really don't want to feel that way again. But really you've got no choice unless you want to jack it in and go and sit in the stand as a spectator.

I had a taste for the buzz of it all and along the way had met some seriously successful people, most of whom had come from nothing. There was no question of me not having another go.

The notion of business failure however has continued to intrigue me and, as my self employed career continued (I went on to found my own publishing company), I came across many entrepreneurs who harboured a dark, terrible secret: a failure in the closet. Nobody ever really talked about it unless it was in the small hours, drunk in a bar and then the unanimous viewpoint was that it made them better, stronger, harder. Almost without exception they had learnt by their mistakes and carried on. In many instances to make more mistakes – but through that white-hot furnace of trial and error they found themselves forged into harder metal. I found it heartening, and often wished that we heard more about these failures because it might encourage more people to have a go if they didn't consider the downside to be so horrific. Sure, there's a difference between a crooked trader or the a director wilfully breaking the law and robbing pensioners of their savings, but there is a genuine army of entrepreneurs out there who have pure motives but just got it slightly wrong. So many things are stacked against you when you start and you never even consider the pitfalls when you're pumped up about your world-dominating, hare-brained scheme.

In many cases the journey that entrepreneurialism takes you on is one of self discovery. In my particular case I found out that what I actually sought was freedom. My objectives today are to fill my time with an activity that provides me with the freedom to conduct my life without interference from anyone. If I make a few bob along the way then that's even better.

I have stayed in media because it changes all the time and lends itself to the fresh, exciting ideas which still come to me almost daily – most of them utterly implausible. Since my time with Rowan and the team at the *Review* I have launched a slightly fruity women's magazine called *Scarlet*, which has become a bit of a hit. At the time of this book going to press I have just completed the sale of that magazine and am embarking on the launch of a new title called *Cosmetic Surgery Magazine*. I have also branched out into online publishing which has limitless possibilities and doesn't involve cutting down lots of trees to make paper. Which is good. And, of course, I have now fulfilled my life long ambition to write a book – which you have very kindly purchased. I hope you enjoyed it and, if you're thinking about having a go, then take my advice and do it. When your allotted 80 years are up and you're on your deathbed you will not regret it. However it works out.

Index